3RD Edition

BEST **TENT**
Camping

MINNESOTA

YOUR CAR-CAMPING GUIDE TO SCENIC BEAUTY, THE SOUNDS
OF NATURE, AND AN ESCAPE FROM CIVILIZATION

Dedicated to Doug "Mr. B" Barkley
and the memories of Boy Scout Troop 22

Best Tent Camping: Minnesota

Copyright © 2005, 2012, and 2018 by Tom Watson
All rights reserved
Published by Menasha Ridge Press
Distributed by Publishers Group West
Printed in the United States of America
Third edition, first printing

Library of Congress Cataloging-in-Publication Data

Names: Watson, Tom, 1947- author.
Title: Best tent camping Minnesota : your car-camping guide to scenic beauty, the sounds of nature, and an escape
    from civilization / Tom Watson .
Description: Third Edition. | Birmingham, AL : Menasha Ridge Press, [2018] | Includes index. | Revised edition of : Best
    in tent camping Minnesota : a guide for car campers who hate RVs, concrete slabs, and loud portable stereos /
    Tom Watson. c2005.
Identifiers: LCCN 2017057618 | ISBN 9781634041249 (pbk.) | ISBN 9781634041256 (ebook)
Subjects: LCSH: Camp sites, facilities, etc.—Minnesota—Guidebooks. | Camping—Minnesota—Guidebooks. |
    Minnesota—Guidebooks.
Classification: LCC GV191.42.M6 W38 2018 | DDC 917.76/068—dc23
LC record available at https://lccn.loc.gov/2017057618

Cover and book design: Jonathan Norberg
Maps: Steve Jones
Project editor: Amber Kaye Henderson
Copy editor: Kate Johnson
Proofreader: Holly Smith
Indexer: Meghan Brawley/Potomac Indexing
All photos by Tom Watson unless otherwise noted

 MENASHA RIDGE PRESS
An imprint of AdventureKEEN
2204 First Ave. S., Ste. 102
Birmingham, AL 35233

Visit menasharidge.com for a complete listing of our books and for ordering information. Contact us at our website, at
facebook.com/menasharidge, or at twitter.com/menasharidge with questions or comments. To find out more about
who we are and what we're doing, visit blog.menasharidge.com.

Front cover: Main photo: High Falls along the Superior Hiking Trail in Tettegouche State Park (see page 82) © Paul D.
Sorenson, Forest City, Iowa
Inset photo: Boundary Waters Canoe Area Wilderness by Dan Thornberg/Shutterstock.com

3RD Edition

BEST TENT
Camping

MINNESOTA

YOUR CAR-CAMPING GUIDE TO SCENIC BEAUTY, THE SOUNDS
OF NATURE, AND AN ESCAPE FROM CIVILIZATION

Tom Watson

MENASHA RIDGE PRESS
Your Guide to the Outdoors Since 1982

Minnesota Campground Locator Map

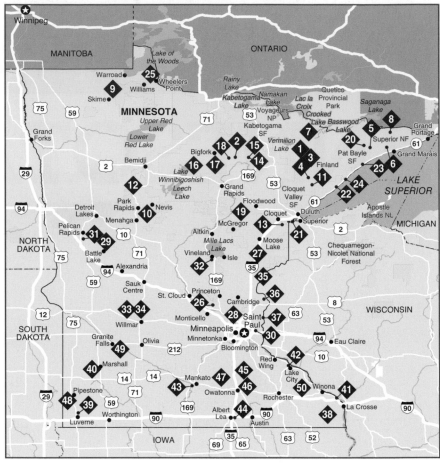

CONTENTS

NORTHERN MINNESOTA 11

CENTRAL MINNESOTA 88

SOUTHERN MINNESOTA 127

Map Legend

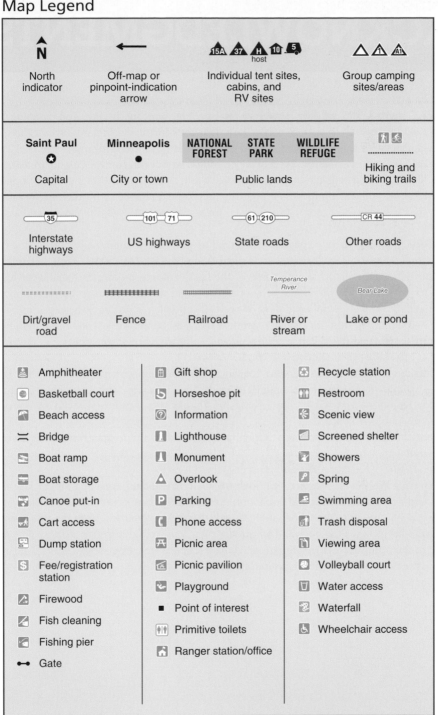

North indicator

Off-map or pinpoint-indication arrow

Individual tent sites, cabins, and RV sites

Group camping sites/areas

Saint Paul ★ — Capital

Minneapolis ● — City or town

NATIONAL FOREST · **STATE PARK** · **WILDLIFE REFUGE** — Public lands

Hiking and biking trails

---

35 — Interstate highways

101 71 — US highways

61 210 — State roads

CR 44 — Other roads

Dirt/gravel road

Fence

Railroad

Temperance River — River or stream

Bear Lake — Lake or pond

Amphitheater	Gift shop	Recycle station
Basketball court	Horseshoe pit	Restroom
Beach access	Information	Scenic view
Bridge	Lighthouse	Screened shelter
Boat ramp	Monument	Showers
Boat storage	Overlook	Spring
Canoe put-in	Parking	Swimming area
Cart access	Phone access	Trash disposal
Dump station	Picnic area	Viewing area
Fee/registration station	Picnic pavilion	Volleyball court
Firewood	Playground	Water access
Fish cleaning	Point of interest	Waterfall
Fishing pier	Primitive toilets	Wheelchair access
Gate	Ranger station/office	

ACKNOWLEDGMENTS

My dad planted the outdoor seeds in me—fishing, hunting, hiking, and camping. By today's standards, our trips were pretty basic, but they instilled a lifelong love of the outdoors. I also spent many a great weekend outdoors in Missouri with my Uncle Dick, my Aunt Rubelle, and my cousins. There were countless wonderful summer nights in tents or, more likely, the old Ford station wagon, where cousin Bruce and I, along with my younger cousin Robin, would sleep restlessly, awaiting dawn and a chance to hit the nearby catfish hole. They were like brothers to me, their house was always my second home—and we all loved to camp! Thank you.

Special thanks goes to the person who taught me not only so many skills but also the values behind them—my Scoutmaster and friend Doug Barkley. He and the gang in Troop 22 in Minneapolis provided me with some of the best camping memories I shall ever have. The sacrifices made by Mr. B and other parents to get the troop out camping can never be repaid. Those were wonderful days of rain-soaked Baker tents, rock-hard ground, and dedicated honing of outdoors skills, regardless of the weather. We learned more than how to camp; we learned self-reliance and confidence, and we learned to respect the outdoors. For that I shall always be indebted to Mr. B.

Thank you, Lynn, my sister, who is always there to help with projects like this, who always has a good idea or an encouraging word. When I wasn't camping out, I was crashing at her place on the way to or from a campsite. Thanks to my mom too, who always supported my outdoor 'venturing!

Special thanks to Bill Morrissey, a friend, college buddy, and former director of Minnesota's state parks for several years. His love of the outdoors and the people who make it all happen is part of his incredible and most respected legacy.

My trips are never complete without my dear friend and traveling sidekick, Craig Swedberg—an ace navigator and copilot on these and so many other flights of fancy.

Last, a big thanks to everyone involved with these campgrounds, from the rangers and staff, who keep things together and who share their love and knowledge of these fantastic areas, to the volunteers—the camp hosts who are there to welcome all who come. And also to you, the reader, who enjoys the miracle of nature.

Thank you all.

—Tom Watson

PREFACE

Although I can't remember my first camping trip, I can certainly remember something from the hundreds since then that I've enjoyed throughout my life. Back in the day, camping was easy: there were fewer parks from which to choose and fewer conveniences. Every site was a "rustic" site, and you didn't expect anything more than a picnic table, a fire ring, and a fairly level patch of ground on which to pitch a tent. It must have left its mark because, even today, with all the options before me, those basic amenities are all that I ever really need to enjoy a campsite.

Picking a finite number of campgrounds to include in a "best of" listing is not an exact science. Are 25 too few, are 100 too many? What's the likelihood one can truly stick to the criteria and actually hit that exact number? What about the 62 best sites, or the 43 best? More important, I feel, is that the criteria remain constant and based on unchanging standards that the author can share with the reader.

Hopefully your awareness of what I look for in a campsite will help you interpret my selections in this book. I grew up loving the outdoors, the wilder places, the less developed areas. I graduated from Minnesota's College of Forestry and have spent 20 years as an occasional naturalist and outdoors writer. I love camping away from the madding crowd, sometimes off the trail and without a tent. Backpack camping is my first love; drive-up camping is a convenient and comfortable second.

Be advised, some state parks offer fantastic natural amenities but bland campsites. Some state forests have wonderful campgrounds—the best in the state—but few other amenities. Voyageurs National Park and the Boundary Waters Canoe Area Wilderness are almost exclusively water-access campsites and were not among those considered for this particular book, although both could provide 50 great campsites at the unfolding of a map. Purposely left out, too, were the scores of backcountry campsites available within the Chippewa and Superior National Forests. Most of these are accessible only by water or at the end of long trails. They offer some of the most remote, pristine, and self-reliant camping in the state.

There is only one private campground listed here (Spirit Mountain; see page 73). Space is money, so private campgrounds tend to either pack 'em in hubcap to trailer hitch or provide a grid of sterile sites on parking lawns with broomstick trees—definitely not my kind of camping.

Still, I must confess, I admire those who at least attempt to enjoy the outdoors at whatever level. It's not so much where you stay while you share in that pleasure, but merely that you go at all. For those of you, however, who appreciate the tent pad and fire ring, who seek the quiet, rustic places—or at least a sense of them—this list of 50 choice campgrounds is for you.

Imagine if, in this state of 10,000 lakes, each of those lakes had a campground beside it? Well, there are actually more than 12,000 bodies of water that qualify as lakes, and a large number of them do indeed have at least one or two campsites nestled about their shorelines. Some of these are accessible only by canoe or other water vessel; some require a lengthy hike over challenging terrain; and some are connected by at least a thread of a roadway. It's those in the last group that are represented in this guide as some of the best tent-camping opportunities in the state.

The interesting and alluring thing about Minnesota, besides those lakes, is the diverse geology and natural character of this northern state. One can enjoy camping in three distinct but overlapping regions: the southeastern Big Woods region, accented by remnant hardwood forests lining deep, glacially carved river valleys; the expansive western region, with the remains and restored segments of the vast prairies and oak savannas that once spread across the middle third of our nation; and the awe-inspiring northern boreal forests of majestic pines, aromatic evergreens, and glimmering birches that blanket the rocky outcrops and islands throughout the northern shore region. These areas are preserved and showcased in hundreds of campgrounds scattered throughout Minnesota.

Most of these campgrounds are gems within a state park, state forest, or national forest jewel box. Some are multifaceted, whereas others seem more like hidden stones as yet unpolished by the jeweler's wheel. Each is representative of other camping opportunities in that region and is therefore listed as an example of what you might expect when you venture out nearby.

The fall colors and blufftop vistas from Great River Bluffs State Park south of Winona to the dog hair–thick clusters of paper birch at Zippel Bay State Park lining the shores of Lake of the Woods are just a few of the wonderful sights awaiting visitors to our state parks. Other campgrounds, such as Temperance River and Tettegouche, showcase thundering waterfalls, and some offer isolated campsites that are the best of the best. Still others are within the seven-county region of the Twin Cities and offer beautiful, rustic sites just off major freeways.

Minnesota's many state forests and two national forests (Chippewa and Superior) offer dense stands of northern conifers and hardwoods amid lakes of all sizes—camping here is a convenience for those who love to hunt and fish in these scattered forest preserves.

Whether you enjoy camping amid the exposed rock shelves of the Canadian Shield at a northern shore campground or amid prairie flowers and the nighttime howl of coyotes in the middle of a western Minnesota grassland, you can be assured that these 50 highlighted campsites will provide you with many summers—and winters—of splendid campsite options.

Each agency offering camping facilities has plenty of information to help you choose and, in some cases, secure a site in advance. Please refer to the information within each listing and the reference list in Appendix B. Whether you head up north, out west, or down south, there are campgrounds awaiting you, no matter what your fancy. Grab your tent and sleeping bag and enjoy.

—Tom Watson

BEST
CAMPGROUNDS

BEST FOR FISHING

BEST FOR HIKING

BEST FOR HORSEBACK RIDING

BEST FOR PADDLING

BEST FOR SWIMMING

BEST FOR WATERFALLS

BEST FOR WILDLIFE VIEWING

INTRODUCTION

HOW TO USE THIS GUIDEBOOK

The publishers of Menasha Ridge Press welcome you to *Best Tent Camping: Minnesota*. Whether you are new to this activity or have been sleeping in your portable outdoor shelter over decades of outdoor adventures, please review the following information. It explains how we have worked with the author to organize this book and how you can make the best use of it.

THE RATINGS AND RATING CATEGORIES

This guidebook's author personally experienced dozens of campgrounds and campsites to select the top 50 locations in this state. Within that universe of 50, the author then ranked each one in the six categories described below. As a tough grader, the author awarded few five-star ratings, but each campground in this guidebook is superlative in its own way. For example, a site may be rated only one star in one category but perhaps five stars in another category. This rating system allows you to choose your destination based on the attributes that are most important to you:

★★★★★   The site is **ideal** in that category.

★★★★   The site is **exemplary** in that category.

★★★   The site is **very good** in that category.

★★   The site is **above average** in that category.

★   The site is **acceptable** in that category.

BEAUTY

Beauty, of course, is in the eye of the beholder, but panoramic views or proximity to a lake or river earn especially high marks. A campground that blends in well with the environment scores well, as do areas with remarkable wildlife or geology. Well-kept vegetation and nicely laid-out sites also up the ratings.

PRIVACY

The number of sites in a campground, the amount of screening between them, and physical distance from one another are decisive factors for the privacy ratings. Other considerations include the presence of nearby trails or day-use areas, and proximity to a town or city that would invite regular day-use traffic and perhaps compromise privacy.

OPPOSITE: The rocky cliff near Big Spring on Beaver Creek (see page 128)

SPACIOUSNESS

The size of the tent spot, its proximity to other tent spots, and whether or not it is defined or bordered from activity areas are the key consideration. The highest ratings go to sites that allow the tent camper to comfortably spread out without overlapping neighboring sites or picnic, cooking, or parking areas.

QUIET

Criteria for this rating include several touchstones: the author's experience at the site, the nearness of roads, the proximity of towns and cities, the probable number of RVs, the likelihood of noisy all-terrain vehicles or boats, and whether a campground host is available or willing to enforce the quiet hours. Of course, one set of noisy neighbors can deflate a five-star rating to a one-star (or no-star), so the latter criterion—campground enforcement—was particularly important in the author's evaluation in this category.

SECURITY

How you determine a campground's security will depend on what you view as the greater risk: other people or the wilderness. The more remote the campground, the less likely you are to run into opportunistic crime but the harder it is to get help in case of an accident or a dangerous wildlife confrontation. Ratings in this category take into consideration whether there is a campground host or resident park ranger, the proximity of other campers' sites, how much day traffic the campground receives, how close the campground is to a town or city, and whether there is cell phone reception or some type of phone or emergency call button.

CLEANLINESS

A campground's appearance often depends on who was there right before you and how your visit coincides with the maintenance schedule. In general, higher marks went to those campgrounds with hosts who cleaned up regularly. The rare case of odor-free toilets also gleaned high marks. At unhosted campgrounds, criteria included the availability of trash receptacles and evidence that sites were cleared and that signs and buildings were kept repaired. Markdowns for the campground were not given for a single visitor's garbage left at a site, but old trash in the shrubbery and along trails, indicating infrequent cleaning, did secure low ratings.

THE CAMPGROUND LOCATOR MAP AND MAP LEGEND

Use the campground locator map on page iv to pinpoint the location of each campground. Each campground's number follows it throughout this guidebook, from the locator map to the table of contents to the profile's first page. A map legend that details the symbols found on the campground-layout maps appears on page vii.

CAMPGROUND-LAYOUT MAPS

Each profile contains a detailed map of campsites, internal roads, facilities, and other key items.

CAMPGROUND ENTRANCE GPS COORDINATES

All 50 profiles in this guidebook include the GPS coordinates for each site entrance. The intersection of the latitude (north) and longitude (west) coordinates orient you at the entrance. Please note that this guidebook uses the degree–decimal minute format for presenting the GPS coordinates. Example:

N47° 47.668'   W92° 4.726'

To convert GPS coordinates from degrees, minutes, and seconds to the above degree–decimal minute format, divide the seconds by 60. For more on GPS technology, visit usgs.gov.

WEATHER

Minnesota's climate is as diverse as its campgrounds. One-quarter of its 80,000 square miles is covered in wetlands and dotted with nearly 12,000 lakes that are more than 10 acres in area. There are nearly 17 million acres of forests throughout the state, from the majestic coniferous stands of white and red pines that make up Minnesota's world-famous north country forests to the vast stands of oak, maple, birch, and other hardwoods throughout the southeastern region and up through the center of the state. Farther west, the expansive prairie grasslands stretch to the Dakota borders.

Each of these biomes has its own distinct weather pattern. Across Minnesota, winter temperatures average about 10°F, while beautiful, blue-sky summer days range in the upper 60s. Campers can count on experiencing rapid shifts in weather patterns that can bring on summer squalls and winter blizzards, sometimes at a moment's notice. At other times, long stretches of mild, soothing weather creates a pleasant camping climate for days on end.

The most common weather elements to prepare for include sustained high winds, especially out on the prairie or throughout the area surrounding and including the Boundary Waters Canoe Area Wilderness. Likewise, torrential downpours can put even the stoutest tent flies and ground cloths to the test—and cause water to rise quickly in floodplains along rivers.

With such varied weather patterns possible throughout the state, a prudent camper should always make sure to bring a variety of clothing and ensure that the campsite is well secured and protected for all possibilities the season might present.

FIRST AID KIT

A useful first aid kit may contain more items than you might think necessary. These are just the basics. Prepackaged kits in waterproof bags are available. As a preventive measure, always take along sunscreen and insect repellent. Always have a list of prescriptions and doses for those in your party who depend on medication. Even though quite a few items are listed here, they pack down into a small space:

- Adhesive bandages
- Antibiotic ointment
- Antiseptic or disinfectant, such as Betadine or hydrogen peroxide

- Benadryl or the generic equivalent, diphenhydramine (*in case of allergic reactions*)
- Butterfly-closure bandages
- Elastic bandages or joint wraps
- Emergency poncho
- Epinephrine in a prefilled syringe (*for severe allergic reactions to bee stings, etc.*)
- Gauze (one roll and six 4-by-4-inch pads)
- Ibuprofen or acetaminophen
- Insect repellent
- LED flashlight or headlamp
- Matches or pocket lighter
- Mirror for signaling passing aircraft
- Moleskin/Spenco 2nd Skin
- Pocketknife or multipurpose tool
- Sunscreen/lip balm
- Waterproof first aid tape
- Whistle (*it's more effective than your voice in signaling rescuers*)

FLORA AND FAUNA PRECAUTIONS

DANGEROUS PLANTS

Poison ivy is ever present in the region's forested parks as well as alongside trails in both country and urban settings. Recognizing and avoiding contact with the plant is the most effective way to prevent the painful, itchy rash it causes. Poison ivy ranges from a thick, tree-hugging vine to a shaded ground cover, three leaflets to a leaf. Urushiol, the oil in the plant's sap, is responsible for the rash. Usually within 12–14 hours of exposure (but sometimes much later), raised lines and/or blisters appear, accompanied by a terrible itch. Refrain from scratching—bacteria under fingernails can cause infection. Wash and dry the rash thoroughly, applying a calamine lotion or similar product to help dry it out. If itching or blistering is severe, seek medical attention. Remember that the oil can contaminate clothes, pets, or hiking gear as well, so wash not only any exposed parts of your body but also anything else that may have come in contact with the plant.

Another nasty plant, stinging nettle, can produce a painful "burn." Learn to identify this tall, tooth-edged, leafy plant as well.

While several species of shrubs, such as the woody hawthorn and the more vinelike raspberry, have thorns, none compare to the prickly mountain ash. Unassuming as it grows along the trail, looking innocently like a small green ash, the prickly ash has needle-sharp thorns ready to bite the hand that grabs it or lash out at an arm or leg that passes too closely.

MOSQUITOES

Mosquitoes are common throughout Minnesota. Rarely, individuals can become infected with the West Nile virus by being bitten by an infected mosquito. Culex mosquitoes, the primary varieties that can transmit the virus to humans, thrive in urban rather than natural areas. They are most prevalent in late summer. Most people infected with West Nile virus have no symptoms of illness, but some may become ill, usually 3–15 days after being bitten.

Wear protective clothing, such as long sleeves, long pants, and socks. Loose-fitting, light-colored clothing is your best defense. Spray clothing with insect repellent. Follow the instructions on the repellent, and take extra care to protect children against these insects.

SNAKES

Rattlesnakes are among the most common venomous snakes in the United States, and hibernation season is typically October–April. The rocky bluffs and outcrops of southeastern Minnesota are home to both the timber rattlesnake and the eastern massasauga. While

photographed by Jane Huber

both are venomous, they are rarely encountered. Rattlesnakes like to bask in the sun and won't bite unless threatened.

However, the snakes you most likely will see while hiking will be nonvenomous species and subspecies. The best rule is to leave all snakes alone, give them a wide berth as you hike past, and make sure any hiking companions (including dogs) do the same.

When hiking, stick to well-used trails, and wear over-the-ankle boots and loose-fitting long pants. Do not step or put your hands beyond your range of detailed visibility, and avoid wandering around in the dark. Step *onto* logs and rocks, never *over* them, and be especially careful when climbing rocks. Always avoid walking through dense brush or willow thickets.

TICKS

Ticks are most common throughout the eastern, south, and central regions of Minnesota, especially in warmer months. They are often found on brush and tall grass, waiting to hitch a ride on a warm-blooded passerby. Adult ticks are most active April–May and again

October–November. Among the varieties of ticks, the black-legged tick, commonly called the deer tick, is the primary carrier of Lyme disease. American dog ticks, or wood ticks, transmit Rocky Mountain spotted fever. Wear light-colored clothing to make it easier for you to spot ticks before they migrate to your skin. Use an insect repellent that contains DEET to help keep them away.

At the end of the hike, visually check your hair, back of neck, armpits, and socks. Ticks prefer places where they're held tightly against the skin, such as elastic on socks and underwear, underarms, waistband, and backs of knees. During your posthike shower, take a moment to do a more complete body check. For ticks that are already embedded, removal with tweezers is best. Grab it as close to the skin surface as possible, and firmly pull it loose without crushing it. Do your best to remove the head, but do not twist. Use disinfectant solution on the wound, and expect a bit of redness and itching for a few days around the bite site.

ROADS AND VEHICLES

Some forest service roads consist of gravel surfaces and are quite narrow, perhaps not suited for larger recreational vehicles or towing larger camping units. Local road closures sometimes occur during excessive rainfall in low-lying areas. Drive cautiously in areas where timber harvest operations are active, especially when encountering large log-hauling trucks on narrow, forested roadways.

PERMITS AND ACCESS

Overnight camping fees vary by agency and even among individual campgrounds within the same unit of government. Daily and seasonal use permits also vary by agency. Most campgrounds provide a drop box for registration and for paying both overnight fees and park permits. Check the campground's profile for fees.

CAMPGROUND ETIQUETTE

Here are a few tips on how to create good vibes with fellow campers and wildlife you encounter.

- **MAKE SURE YOU CHECK IN,** pay your fee, and mark your site as directed. Don't make the mistake of grabbing a seemingly empty site that looks more appealing than your site. It could be reserved. If you're unhappy with the site you've selected, check with the campground host for other options.

- **BE SENSITIVE TO THE GROUND BENEATH YOU.** Be sure to place all garbage in designated receptacles, or pack it out if none is available. No one likes to see the trash someone else has left behind.

- **IT'S COMMON FOR ANIMALS TO WANDER THROUGH CAMPSITES,** where they may be accustomed to the presence of humans (and our food). An unannounced approach, a sudden movement, or a loud noise startles most animals. A surprised animal can be dangerous to you, to others, and to itself. Give them plenty of space.

- **PLAN AHEAD.** Know your equipment, your ability, and the area where you are camping—and prepare accordingly. Be self-sufficient at all times; carry necessary supplies for changes in weather or other conditions. A well-executed trip is a satisfaction to you and to others.

- **BE COURTEOUS TO OTHER CAMPERS,** hikers, bikers, and anyone else you encounter. Be aware of sound levels when talking, playing music, and so on.

- **STRICTLY FOLLOW THE CAMPGROUND'S RULES** regarding the building of fires. Never burn trash. Trash smoke smells horrible, and trash debris in a fire pit or grill is unsightly.

- **FIREWOOD IS A PRIME CARRIER OF FOREST PESTS** into new areas and can harbor many kinds of invasive pests that are harmful to Minnesota trees. Minnesota forests are at particular risk from the emerald ash borer.

- **WHEN CAMPING OR PICNICKING,** obtain your firewood only from Department of Natural Resources–approved vendors near your destination. Keep your receipt to show proof of purchase. In some campgrounds, certified wood is available on-site. See the campground host for more information.

- **NEVER LEAVE YOUR CAMPFIRE UNATTENDED.**

THE JOY OF CAMPING

There is nothing worse than a bad camping trip, especially because it is so easy to have a great time. To assist with making your outing a pleasant and fulfilling one, here are some pointers:

- **RESERVE YOUR SITE IN ADVANCE,** especially if it's a weekend or a holiday, or if the campground is wildly popular. Many prime campgrounds require at least a six-month lead time on reservations. Check before you go.

- **PICK YOUR CAMPING BUDDIES WISELY.** Camping experience and comfort with the outdoors can vary greatly among friends and family members. After you know who's going, make sure that everyone is on the same page regarding expectations of difficulty (amenities or the lack thereof, physical exertion, and so on), sleeping arrangements, and food requirements.

- **DON'T DUPLICATE EQUIPMENT,** such as cooking pots and lanterns, among campers in your party. Carry what you need to have a good time, but don't turn the trip into a cross-country moving experience. Assess the quality and appropriateness of equipment being brought by less experienced campers.

- **DRESS FOR THE SEASON.** Educate yourself on the temperature highs and lows of the specific part of the state you plan to visit. It may be warm at night in the summer in your backyard, but along the northern lakeshores it may be quite chilly. Make sure all clothing is made out of materials appropriate for the conditions you might encounter.

- **PITCH YOUR TENT ON A LEVEL SURFACE**, preferably one covered with leaves, pine straw, or grass. Use a tarp or specially designed footprint to thwart ground moisture and to protect the tent floor. Do a little site maintenance, such as picking up the small rocks and sticks that can damage your tent floor and make sleep uncomfortable. If you have a separate rain fly but don't think you'll need it, consider putting it up anyway, just in case it starts raining at midnight.

  Consider taking a sleeping pad if the ground makes you uncomfortable. Choose a pad that is full-length and thicker than you think you might need. This will not only keep your hips from aching on hard ground but will also help keep you warm. A wide range of thin, light, and inflatable pads is available at camping stores, and these are a much better choice than home air mattresses, which conduct heat away from the body and tend to deflate during the night.

  If you are not hiking to a primitive campsite, there is no real need to skimp on food due to weight. Plan tasty meals and bring everything you will need to prepare, cook, eat, and clean up.

- **IF YOU TEND TO USE THE BATHROOM AT NIGHT,** you should plan ahead. Leaving a warm sleeping bag and stumbling around in the dark to find the restroom—whether it be a pit toilet, a fully plumbed comfort station, or just the woods—is not fun. Keep a flashlight and any other accoutrements you

Wildflower meadow high above the Mississippi River Valley in Great River Bluffs State Park (see page 137)

may need (an umbrella perhaps?) by the tent door, and know exactly where to head in the dark.

- **STANDING DEAD TREES** and storm-damaged living trees can pose a real hazard to tent campers. These trees may have loose or broken limbs that could fall at any time. When choosing a campsite or even just a spot to rest during a hike, look up.

A WORD ABOUT BACKCOUNTRY CAMPING

Following these guidelines will increase your chances for a pleasant, safe, and low-impact interaction with nature.

- **ADHERE TO THE ADAGES** "Pack it in, pack it out" and "Take only pictures, leave only footprints." Practice Leave No Trace camping ethics (visit lnt.org /learn/seven-principles-overview for details) while in the backcountry.

- **IN MINNESOTA, OPEN FIRES ARE PERMITTED** except during dry times when the forest service may issue a fire ban. Backpacking stoves are strongly encouraged. Fire danger levels are usually posted at local Department of Natural Resources offices throughout the state.

- **HANG FOOD AWAY FROM BEARS** and other animals to prevent them from becoming introduced to (and dependent on) human food. Wildlife learns to associate backpacks and backpackers with easy food sources, thereby influencing their behavior.

- **ALWAYS USE BEAR/CRITTER BOXES** for food storage; they are there for good reason. Because children often wipe food from their hands onto their clothing, tossing those garments, smeared with food odors, into the corner of your tent invites trouble from hungry animals. Campgrounds typically post warnings of any current animal threats in the area.

- **BURY SOLID HUMAN WASTE** in a hole at least 3 inches deep and at least 200 feet away from trails and water sources; a trowel is basic backpacking equipment. More and more often, however, the practice of burying human waste is being banned. Using a portable latrine (which comes in various incarnations— basically a glorified plastic bag—and may be given out by park rangers) may seem unthinkable at first, but it's really no big deal. Just bring an extralarge zip-top plastic bag for additional insurance against structural failures.

VENTURING AWAY FROM THE CAMPGROUND

If you go for a hike, bike ride, or other excursion into any remote, backcountry area, keep these precautions in mind:

- **ALWAYS CARRY FOOD AND WATER,** whether you are planning to go overnight or not. Food will give you energy, help keep you warm, and sustain you in an emergency until help arrives. Bring potable water or treat water by boiling or filtering before drinking from any natural water source.

- **STAY ON DESIGNATED TRAILS.** Most hikers get lost when they leave the trail. Even on the most clearly marked trails, there is usually a point where you have to stop and consider which direction to head. If you become disoriented, don't panic. As soon as you think you may be off-track, stop, assess your current direction, and then retrace your steps back to the point where you went awry. If you have absolutely no idea how to continue, return to the trailhead the way you came in. Should you become completely lost and have no idea of how to return to the trailhead, remaining in place along the trail and waiting for help is most often the best option for adults and always the best option for children.

- **ALWAYS CARRY A WHISTLE.** Its shrill sound carries for a long distance, and you can maintain that sound signal much longer than you can continue hollering.

- **BE ESPECIALLY CAREFUL WHEN CROSSING STREAMS.** Whether you're fording the stream or crossing on a log, make every step count. If you have any doubt about maintaining your balance on a log, go ahead and ford the stream instead. When fording a stream, use a trekking pole or stout stick for balance, and face upstream as you cross. If a stream seems too deep to ford, turn back. Whatever is on the other side is not worth risking your life. Be sure your footwear is solid but removable if your foot becomes lodged in a rock or other obstruction below the surface.

- **BE CAREFUL AT OVERLOOKS.** Though these areas may provide spectacular views, they are potentially hazardous. Stay back from the edge of outcrops, and be absolutely sure of your footing: a misstep can mean a nasty and possibly fatal fall.

- **KNOW THE SYMPTOMS OF HYPOTHERMIA.** Shivering, forgetfulness, and unsteadiness are the most common indicators of this insidious killer. Hypothermia can occur at any elevation, and even in the summer. Wearing cotton clothing puts you especially at risk because cotton, when wet, wicks heat away from the body. To prevent hypothermia, dress in layers, using synthetic clothing for insulation; use a cap and gloves to reduce heat loss; and protect yourself with waterproof, breathable outerwear. If symptoms arise, get the victim to shelter, a fire, hot liquids, and dry clothes or a dry sleeping bag.

- **TAKE ALONG YOUR BRAIN.** A cool, calculating mind is the single most important piece of equipment you'll ever need on the trail. Think before you act. Watch your step. Plan ahead. Avoiding accidents before they happen is the best recipe for a rewarding and relaxing hike.

NORTHERN MINNESOTA

photographed by Lisa A. Crayford

Lower falls just above Lower Campground in Temperance River State Park (see page 79)

Bear Head Lake State Park Campground

Beauty ★★★★★ / Privacy ★★★ / Spaciousness ★★★ / Quiet ★★★ / Security ★★★ / Cleanliness ★★★★

Hilly, winding roads through towering pines and a beautiful sky-blue lake make this an especially impressive north-country park.

Nestled amid the lakes within Minnesota's Bear Island State Forest, Bear Head Lake State Park's entrance is a journey along a winding, undulating road through dense, pristine stands of towering red pines. My immediate and lasting impression as I drove the 6.8 miles into this park from the highway was that I was back at Lake Itasca. After my visit, however, I can say this park is beholden to no other—it's a gem unto itself.

The 674-acre lake sits within an expansive forest in glaciated lake country. Bear Head Lake's waters consist of the large main body of the lake and two distinct bays: East and North. These bays are separated by a large, broad peninsula on which the campground complex has been developed. The lake features scores of smaller bays and coves, resulting in a woodsy, irregular shoreline. Several remote, water-access camping sites give backcountry canoe campers and backpackers several options to experience the lake beyond the roadways.

Of the three elongated loops along which campsites are located, the first section, featuring sites 1–24, is probably best suited for tent campers (as opposed to RVs and trailers). Sites are well spaced and separated by a lush understory that creates privacy between campsites. That said, these sites are fairly close to the roadway and thereby fairly exposed to all campground traffic—pedestrian and vehicular.

Boat access across from the campground at Bear Head Lake

KEY INFORMATION

ADDRESS: 9301 Bear Head State Park Road, Ely, MN 55731

CONTACT: 218-235-2520, dnr.state.mn.us /state_parks/bear_head_lake

OPERATED BY: Minnesota DNR, Division of Parks and Recreation

OPEN: Year-round (water/showers open mid-May–early October)

SITES: 73, 4 backpack-in, 2 canoe-in, 5 camper cabins, 1 guesthouse, 1 group

EACH SITE HAS: Open tent area, picnic table, fire ring

WHEELCHAIR ACCESS: Sites 9 and 65 and 2 camper cabins

ASSIGNMENT: Reservations required (same-day reservations available)

REGISTRATION: Reserve at 866-85-PARKS (72757) or tinyurl.com/mnspreservations

FACILITIES: Restrooms, seasonal showers, vault toilets, water, RV sanitation station

PARKING: 1 vehicle/site

FEES: $23/night summer season, $17/night off-season, $31/night electric sites, $7 daily permit, $35 annual permit, $8.50 reservation fee

---

RESTRICTIONS:

PETS: On 6-foot leash; attended at all times

QUIET HOURS: 10 p.m.–8 a.m.

FIRES: In fire rings; gathering firewood not permitted; firewood must be purchased from approved vendor

ALCOHOL: Not permitted

OTHER: 6 people/site; closed to visitors 10 p.m.–8 a.m.; fireworks and metal detectors prohibited

Sites 1–5 are surrounded by a dense understory, highlighted by a few towering red pines, particularly the stately trees at 4 and 5. The next dozen sites (site 9 is wheelchair accessible) are all fairly small and very close to the roadway, but like the others, they are screened from one another by a buffer of understory beneath more pines and a mixture of spruce and the occasional aspen. Sites 18–24 are just as woodsy, but the driveways are nearly as wide as the campsites themselves, exposing the entire setting to passersby. Sites 12–16 are closest to the lake and near a trail spur at the head of the loop that connects to the Beach Trail.

The second loop finds campsites 25–50 clustered more tightly along the loop; each has electricity, making this and the third loop most popular among those with campers and other RV units. The sites are also well screened but more concentrated along the loop. Several of the smaller sites would serve as adequate tent sites too. Perhaps because of the longer driveways needed to accommodate a camper vehicle, these sites are set back a bit farther from the road.

Sites 51–73 are the closest to the lake (site 65 is wheelchair accessible), but all are on the forest side of the roadway—no sites are located along the lakeshore side. The trees aren't as dense throughout this loop, but that's a big plus, as some sites have a view of the lake. Sites 51–57 are closest to the lake, offering fairly open campsites. The head of this loop, just past site 57, serves as the trailhead for the Beach Trail, which follows the shoreline and continues past the first loop, connecting trail walkers with fishing docks and eventually the picnic and swimming area at a point on Bear Head Lake where the North and East Bays connect to the larger body of water.

The views from the lake are breathtaking. Well-groomed open areas provide campers with myriad opportunities to stop and enjoy the views. Hikers have 14 miles of trails, including access to the Taconite State Trail, which crosses the northern section of the park.

Paddlers and anglers can enjoy miles of undeveloped shoreline surrounding pristine waters teeming with walleye, crappie, bass, and trout.

Nearby Ely (20 miles east) is the gateway to the Boundary Waters Canoe Area Wilderness and offers a wide variety of amenities, including canoe and gear rental and supplies.

Bear Head Lake State Park Campground

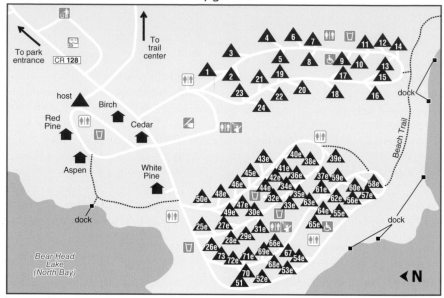

GETTING THERE

From Ely take MN 169 west about 12.5 miles to CR 128/Bear Head State Park Road, and turn left (south). Go 6.8 miles to the park office. From Tower take MN 169 east about 9 miles to CR 128/Bear Head State Park Road, and turn right (south). Go 6.8 miles to the park office.

GPS COORDINATES: N47° 47.668' W92° 4.726'

Bear Lake Campground

Beauty ★★★★ / Privacy ★★★ / Spaciousness ★★★★ / Quiet ★★★ / Security ★★★ / Cleanliness ★★★★

At first it appears to be a big picnic area, but on closer inspection this campground offers a tranquil, lakeside camping retreat.

Bear Lake (not to be confused with Bear Head Lake, farther north) is one of two campgrounds selected within the George Washington State Forest. Situated in the upper corner of Itasca County, the uplands are forested and covered in the predominant species—red, white, and jack pine; two common evergreens, white spruce and balsam fir; and hardwoods (mostly paper birch and aspen). The lowlands are characterized by marshes and bogs, with tamarack and black spruce making up the patches of trees throughout these areas. Northern white cedar, along with elm and ash, also add to the woodsy appeal of these areas.

This campground was developed in the midst of a marshy area—at least that's the impression one gets driving to the campsite. Bear Lake Campground is like a dry, forested oasis amid marshy, reed-lined bogs and other lowland vegetation. Like many other campgrounds in this region, Bear Lake was developed by the Civilian Conservation Corps.

It's a simple campground, laid out like a dog bone along the northern shore of Bear Lake. Most of the sites are spacious throughout the loop, so the deciding factors are privacy and proximity to the lake.

Site 19's view of Bear Lake

KEY INFORMATION

ADDRESS: 55334 W. Bear Lake Forest Road, Cook, MN 55723

CONTACT: 218-743-3362, dnr.state.mn.us /state_forests/facilities/cmp00019

OPERATED BY: Minnesota DNR, Division of Forestry (managed by Scenic State Park)

OPEN: Year-round

SITES: 26

EACH SITE HAS: Open tent area, picnic table, fire ring

WHEELCHAIR ACCESS: Sites 15 and 17

ASSIGNMENT: First come, first served; no reservations

REGISTRATION: Required; envelopes provided

FACILITIES: Vault toilet, water, picnic pavilion

PARKING: 1 vehicle/site

FEES: $14/night

RESTRICTIONS:

PETS: On leash

QUIET HOURS: 10 p.m.–8 a.m.

FIRES: In fire rings; gathering downed or dead firewood permitted; firewood must be purchased from approved vendor

ALCOHOL: Not permitted

OTHER: 8 people/site; hunting and firearms only in posted areas; camping possible in undeveloped areas (special rules apply); check information station for seasonal and special restrictions

Site 1 is very spacious but completely open—just to the right of the entrance to the campground. It sits in a large triangle formed by the campground road, a private road leading off to cabins along the lake, and the lakeshore itself.

Site 2 is the closest campsite to the lake—very beautiful, a "great site," as my notes proclaim. Nestled in red pines mixed with spruce, the site itself is fairly open, but if campers turn their backs on the road, there is only the lake beyond the shore to enjoy.

Site 3 is also on the lake. Although not as spacious as site 2, it's a keeper as well. Because the road turns back in from the lake after site 3, there is quite a bit of distance between this site and site 5 just a bit farther down the road on the lakeside.

Sites 4 is big and situated on the inside of the loop right as the road turns back more parallel to the lake. Site 6 is a big, open site shaded by a stand of pines. It has a large grassy pad for pitching a tent.

Site 7 is a big open square, very near the water, and it offers an exposed grassy site for camping. Likewise, site 8 is exposed. Sites 9–11 are all grouped near the swimming area and offer minimal privacy at moderately sized campsites—take your pick!

Sites 12 and 13 are along the outside curve of the loop but still close to the lake. At site 14, however, the road enters the wooded area and leads to sites that are separated by the trees and understory from the lake. A vault toilet is tucked in between sites 14 and 15.

Sites 15 and 16 are located where the loop swings left. Sites 17, 18, and 20 are average-size sites offering the standard amenities and are just a short walk away from the lake and the swimming area. Both sites 15 and 17 are wheelchair accessible.

Site 19 is a very open site, one you can look through to see down to the lake. It's a fair distance away from another utility hub (vault toilet and water pump). The remaining sites are staggered along opposite sides of the roadway. Site 24 is back beyond the large grassy area that includes the pavilion right inside the campground entrance. The last site in the campground is 26. It may be the least desirable site in the camp, but at least it's tucked into the woods.

The pavilion area is not for camping; it's designed for day use. Groups could play baseball in one section and yard games in another while a third group enjoyed a picnic on the grounds—and no one would be in another's way. Other features include swimming, fishing, a boat ramp, and a large picnic area.

Bear Lake, like many of these northern lakes, is loaded with bass, trout, walleye, panfish, and northern pike. A short walk back out through the entrance and down the gravel road to the east leads to the picnic area and boat ramp for Bear Lake. There are several cabins along the lake to the west of the campground. This campground offers several spacious lakeside sites, all in a groomed, picnic-ground setting.

Bear Lake Campground

GETTING THERE

From Nashwauk take MN 65 north 23 miles to CR 52. Turn left (west) and go 2 miles to CR 552. Turn left (south) and go 3.3 miles, then keep right at the Y onto West Bear Lake Forest Road. The two campground entrances are next on the left.

GPS COORDINATES: N47° 40.672' W93° 16.049'

3

Birch Lake Campground

Beauty ★★★ / Privacy ★★★ / Spaciousness ★★★ / Quiet ★★★ / Security ★★★ / Cleanliness ★★★

This popular fishing campsite is tucked deep into the national forest on a waterway that includes the South Kawishiwi River.

Campers who love to fish will enjoy the angling opportunities at Birch Lake. The lake is considered one of the more productive ones in this part of the forest. Its shallow, 25-foot depth and rocky and irregular shoreline provide an ideal habitat for walleye, smallmouth bass, crappie, northern pike, and panfish. The 5,628-acre reservoir is part of a flowage that includes three other lakes.

That being said, it follows that this is a popular lake for motorized fishing boats (currently there are no horsepower restrictions). Because half the campsites are very near the lake and each has direct access to the water, expect noise to be a factor during the fishing season.

The area where the campground is located is covered in mixed hardwoods. The sites are laid out along two loops, although only half of the northern loop has campsites. The southern loop, laid out in a kidney bean shape, offers a full circle of campsites.

Beginning with site 1 (wheelchair accessible) in the northern loop, the surroundings are a bit sparse; the site sits amid older aspens intermixed with red and white pines. It's a basic site with standard amenities. Site 2 sits inside the loop, is small, and is in a stand of scrub poplars. Site 3 (wheelchair accessible) is lakeside and sits in a low-lying area. Like site 1, this spot has a direct trail down to the lake. In fact, all the sites on the lakeside are connected to the lake by a pathway leading from each campsite.

Site 4 is one of the closest sites to the lakeshore, while 5, inside the loop again, is set back into the woods. Sites 6 (wheelchair accessible) and 7 have a nice overview of the lake—only

Boat access and dock at Birch Lake Campground

KEY INFORMATION

ADDRESS: 11580 Little Lake Road, Ely, MN 55731

CONTACT: Concessionaire: 218-365-2963, camprrm.com/parks/birch-lake-camp-ground; Kawishiwi Ranger District: 218-235-1299, tinyurl.com/birchlake campground

OPERATED BY: Superior National Forest, Kawishiwi Ranger District (managed by Recreation Resource Management)

OPEN: Mid-May–September (no services or fees in winter)

SITES: 28, 1 group

EACH SITE HAS: Open tent area, picnic table, fire ring

WHEELCHAIR ACCESS: Sites 1, 3, and 6

ASSIGNMENT: 17 reservable, 11 first come, first served

REGISTRATION: Fee station at entrance; reserve at 877-444-6777 or recreation.gov

FACILITIES: Vault toilet, water, Dumpster, wheelchair-accessible facilities, boat landing

PARKING: 1 vehicle/site; half fee/additional vehicle at site; also at boat ramp

FEES: $15 daily permit

RESTRICTIONS:

PETS: Under owner's control at all times

QUIET HOURS: 10 p.m.–6 a.m.

FIRES: In fire rings; gathering of downed or dead firewood permitted; firewood must be purchased from approved vendor; non-ash firewood gathered within 100 miles of Superior National Forest permitted

ALCOHOL: Permitted

OTHER: 9 people/site; noise limits enforced at developed sites

---

about 20 yards away at site 6. Sites 8, 9, and 11, all on the inside of the loop, are rather basic and nondescript. The space for your tent is very small and limited at site 10, although it is close to the lake. The remaining three spots in this area are all cut into old-growth aspen (the typical forest throughout the entire campground). Sites 2–12 are first come, first served, so if you want one of these sites for your tent-camping pleasure, get here early. Although site 14 sits on a knoll, this campground's setting is more of a lowland area, such as that found in pockets throughout the north woods—particularly where aspens dominate the forest.

The southern loop features 15 campsites, 9 of which are a short trail section away from the lake. Site 17 is right behind the parking lot for the boat ramp—perhaps convenient but probably noisy with traffic throughout the fishing season. Site 18 is right down on the lake but is very small. Give up space and take the privacy. Site 19 is also nicely located on the lake and was probably designed as an RV site because of its size and the length of its driveway. I thought it was one of the nicest sites in the whole campground.

By site 20, the road is curving back away from the lake, so the rest of the lakeside sites require you to walk a bit farther to the shoreline. Site 21 is situated on a rise above the roadway, accessed by a stairway heading up from a turnout parking space along the campground road.

The next few sites are 23 (long and narrow), 24 (too funky, in the undergrowth, with hardly any room for a tent), 25 (long driveway but small, gravelly tent space near picnic table), and 26 (featuring a long, narrow driveway through a stand of balsam firs). It, too, has a pathway to the lake.

Vegetation blocks the view into site 27, while site 28 sits back in the woods at the top of a short stairway. Sites 29–32 are fairly open, average sites. Of these, only site 29 has direct access to the lake.

If fishing is a big part of your camping agenda, Birch Lake—motorboats and all—is probably a good choice. An irregular shoreline along shallow, rocky bays makes for good canoeing and kayaking as well.

Because of its proximity to Ely and the surrounding back roads laced along and through the Boundary Waters Canoe Area Wilderness, Birch Lake campground is truly a great stop-over site to wet a line and warm up with a few canoe strokes in those shallow, rock-bottom bays where the power boaters can't go.

Birch Lake Campground

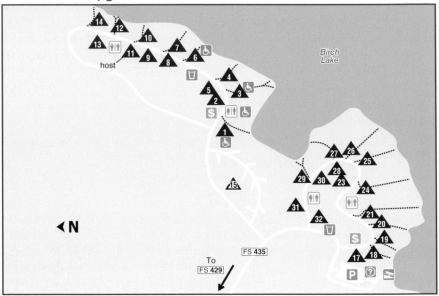

GETTING THERE

From Ely go south 7.9 miles on MN 1 to FS 429/Little Lake Road (look for Birch Camp road sign). Turn right (south) and go 3.5 miles to the campground's entrance road (FS 435) on the left. The campground is 1 mile down this road.

GPS COORDINATES: N47° 45.515′ W91° 47.119′

4

Cadotte Lake Campground

Beauty ★★ / Privacy ★★★★ / Spaciousness ★★★★ / Quiet ★★★ / Security ★★★ / Cleanliness ★★★

This modest campground was cut out of a rough, northern boreal forest and offers lake swimming and fishing.

Cadotte Lake is one of several Superior National Forest campgrounds clustered in a mature northern boreal forest some 20-plus miles inland from Lake Superior. Like others listed, Cadotte Lake can be looked at as an alternative to the more developed parks that line the North Shore of Lake Superior. Also, its proximity to the southern boundaries of the Boundary Waters Canoe Area Wilderness make this and other campgrounds good layover sites when that push from southern Minnesota gets to be a bit too long. Of course, Cadotte Lake offers a quaint retreat, featuring swimming and fishing in a remote, spacious, private campground.

Cadotte Lake shoreline

KEY INFORMATION

ADDRESS: Bundle Lake Road, 1.5 miles west of Town Line Road, Brimson, MN 55602

CONTACT: 218-229-8800, tinyurl.com /cadottelakecg; 218-410-9098, camprrm .com/parks/cadotte-lake

OPERATED BY: Superior National Forest, Laurentian Ranger District (managed by Recreation Resource Management)

OPEN: Year-round (facilities: early May– November; no services or fees in winter)

SITES: 26

EACH SITE HAS: Open tent area, picnic table, fire ring

WHEELCHAIR ACCESS: No designated sites

ASSIGNMENT: 16 first come, first served; 10 reservable

REGISTRATION: Fee station at entrance; reserve at 877-444-6777 or recreation.gov

FACILITIES: Well, wheelchair-accessible hydrant, vault toilets, boat launch

PARKING: 1 vehicle/site; $8/additional vehicle at site; also at boat ramp and between campground loops

FEES: $19/night single, $21/night premium (water access, view)

RESTRICTIONS:

PETS: Under owner's control at all times

QUIET HOURS: 10 p.m.–6 a.m.

FIRES: In fire rings; gathering of downed or dead firewood permitted; firewood must be purchased from approved vendor; non-ash firewood gathered within 100 miles of Superior National Forest permitted

ALCOHOL: Permitted

OTHER: 9 people/site; noise limits enforced at developed sites

The camp is laid out in a double loop that parallels Cadotte Lake, giving half the sites direct access to the water. The swimming beach is located just off the boat launching area, and a fishing deck is located a little more than halfway down from loop 1 yet is easily accessible via a trail from the main campground loop road.

There are 12 sites in loop 1, 5 of which are lakeside with their own pathway down to the shore. All these sites are set into a northern boreal forest consisting mostly of spruce, fir, and aspen in various stages of growth. The dominant understory vegetation is alder, which combines with other understory growth to provide a dense screen between the sites.

Site 2 is a good example of the campsites at Cadotte Lake: an expanded opening for a campsite at the end of a long, narrow driveway—keyhole shaped. Like all the campsites, this one features the standard picnic table, tent site, and fire ring. The long driveway and dense understory make this otherwise very open site quite private.

Site 3 is an open site, and 4 (the campground host) is positioned between the vault toilets and the accessible hydrant—too many utilities too close by for my taste. Like site 3, site 5 has a trail leading down to the lake, as do all the other spots on the lake side of both loops. Site 8 is a large site off by itself, seemingly private except it appears to be way too close to site 10 (the smallest site in this circle).

Site 11 is the last site on this loop with direct access to the lake (only about 30 yards away). Site 12 completes the loop and is a spacious, open site in a wooded area that appears more natural and less manicured than many of the forests in most campgrounds. This is typical of mixed-age aspen forests, right down to the varying sizes and ages of the balsam firs that are really more understory in this section.

The second loop offers 15 campsites, 5 of which are along the lake. Sites 13 and 14 are long, narrow sites. They back up to site 25, limiting privacy. Site 15 is a long, narrow site that would be inviting for an RV. Site 16 is a small spot that backs up to site 20 on the lake side of the loop.

Site 17 is at the end of about a 10-yard trail, setting this camping area off by itself. It's at the end of the second loop and so enjoys an extra amount of privacy deep in the woods. Site 18 is another long and narrow site.

Site 19 has a few boulders and clusters of balsam fir around it (a nice North Shore touch). A short trail along the shoreline to the far end of loop 1 begins at site 19. Sites 20–22 are likewise within this stand of mixed-age fir. Sites 23 and 29 are especially nice for this campground.

The fishing pier tests anglers' ability to catch northern pike, walleye, and panfish. Swimming, boating, hiking, boat rentals, and bait are available too.

Major services are available in Hoyt Lakes, about 12 miles northwest of the campground.

Cadotte Lake Campground

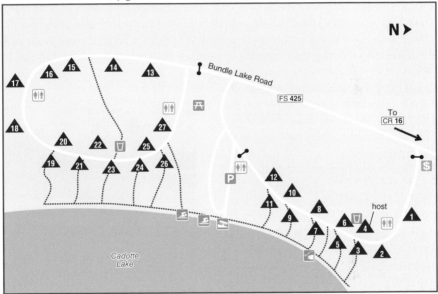

GETTING THERE

From the intersection of MN 61 and Fourth Street/CR 2 in Two Harbors, take Fourth Street/CR 2 north 13 miles to Wales Road/CR 14. Turn left (west) and drive about 10 miles to Rollins (CR 14 becomes Two Harbors–Brimson Road/CR 55 at about 7.7 miles). At Rollins take Brimson Road/CR 44 north (right) 7 miles to Fairbanks Road. Turn left (west), and in 1 mile turn right (north) onto CR 44/FS 1821. In 2 miles turn left (west) onto Town Line Road/CR 16. Go 1.4 miles to Bundle Lake Road/CR 804/FS 425. Turn right and go 0.5 mile, then turn left to stay on Bundle Lake Road for 1 mile to the campground.

GPS COORDINATES: N47° 22.829' W91° 55.010'

Crescent Lake Campground

Beauty ★★★★ / Privacy ★★★★★ / Spaciousness ★★★★ / Quiet ★★★ / Security ★★★★ / Cleanliness ★★★★

This campground winds along a beautiful, island-speckled lake and has some of the state's best primitive lakeside walk-in sites.

Finally, a campground that's not a boilerplate layout! Instead, it's a crescent-shaped line of campsites that follows the irregular shoreline of the lake and the undulating curves of the surrounding topography. It is unique among all the campgrounds I visited, offering not only spacious drive-up sites but also seven of the more inviting walk-in sites in Minnesota. Yes, I love this campground!

Crescent Lake lies just east of the Sawbill Trail and just outside the boundaries of the Boundary Waters Canoe Area Wilderness. You have the perfect hideaway here on this 755-acre lake with all its little rocky islands and tall, moss-covered evergreens along the shoreline. It is a motorboat lake, and that is a drawback for purists who don't want to see or hear such mechanization during their camping experience. Still, this is a great spot to play hide-and-don't-seek camping with your neighbors.

These campsites retain more individuality than most others in the state. There are two camping areas: the stretch along the road paralleling the lake and the units right next to the boat launching area.

The first site along the main campground entrance road is site 10, a few hundred yards past the road to the boat launching area. It sits above the long, narrow driveway on a knoll overlooking the road. This is a very private site, nearly isolated from the road and definitely isolated from everything and everyone else in this park. Whereas site 10 is appealing, site 11 is plain, small, ordinary, and close to the road.

Sites 12–14 are staggered and cut into the woods either above or below the roadway and are accessible by short stairways leading from the vehicle turnouts. Site 15 is very open and on a level piece of ground. Sites 16 and 17 are both on terraces above the road, and each has a stairway leading to the picnic table, fire ring, and tent space that serve as the amenities for this and all sites.

This entire stretch of forest is dominated by fir trees strewn with mosslike tinsel on a Christmas tree. Sites 16 and 17 sit amid the firs, each situated above the roadway; 17 sits

Small rocky island in Crescent Lake

KEY INFORMATION

ADDRESS: Forest Route 1274, 1 mile south of FS 170 (also noted as FS 165 or The Grade on maps), Lutsen, MN 55612

CONTACT: Concessionaire: 218-663-7150, sawbill.com/www/campgrounds/crescent; Tofte Ranger District: 218-663-8060, tinyurl.com/crescentlakecampground

OPERATED BY: Superior National Forest, Tofte Ranger District (managed by Sawbill Canoe Outfitters)

OPEN: Year-round (facilities: May–October; no fees or services in winter)

SITES: 26 rustic, 7 walk-in

EACH SITE HAS: Open tent area, picnic table, fire ring

WHEELCHAIR ACCESS: Site 9; wheelchair access to fishing pier

ASSIGNMENT: 17 reservable; 16 first come, first served

REGISTRATION: Fee station inside loop

across from site 31; reserve at 877-444-6777 or recreation.gov

FACILITIES: Vault toilet, water, trash containers, boat access and storage, parking area, barrier-free fishing pier

PARKING: 1 vehicle/site; $9/additional vehicle at site (must park on spur); also at boat ramp and campground pavilion

FEES: $18/night

RESTRICTIONS:

PETS: Under owner's control at all times

QUIET HOURS: 10 p.m.–6 a.m.

FIRES: In fire rings; gathering of downed or dead firewood permitted; firewood must be purchased from approved vendor; non-ash firewood gathered within 100 miles of Superior National Forest permitted

ALCOHOL: Permitted

OTHER: 9 people/site; 14-day stay limit; noise limits are enforced at developed sites; fireworks prohibited

---

away from the road, too, and is eight or nine steps from it. Site 18 is even farther up off the roadway. It sits on a crest overlooking the lake (a strained view through the trees) and is at least 15 steps above the parking area next to the road.

There's more of the same at sites 19 (requires a climb of more than 20 steps), 20 (situated just above the road), 21, and 22. Pete's Point Trail starts (or finishes) at a trailhead right across the road from the turnout to site 22. This short trail makes its way down to the lake, out to—you guessed it—Pete's Point, and then back again, connecting with the road just past site 17.

Site 23 has a permanent camp "resident" in the form of a giant, 4-foot-high boulder just beyond the picnic table. Site 26 is one of the first sites that is really close to the water and is laid out along the shoreline. Several small, tree-covered, rocky islands are just offshore beginning at this site. It and its faraway next-tent-flap neighbor, site 29, are two of the best spots in the drive-up area for grand views of the lake from camp. Sites 27 and 28 sit on the opposite side of the road from the lake and are cut way back into the woods, barely visible from the road.

The last four sites in this section are laid out along the outside edge of a cul-de-sac. Small site 30 sits right on the edge of the road. These are not very large sites—more typical of sites in other parks. Site 33 did not appear to have a level spot to pitch a tent. Its uneven ground makes it more suitable for an RV rig and is used as the campground host site.

The other section of campground is located next to the boat launch and actually consists of two groups of campsites: drive-up sites 6–9 and walk-in sites 1–5 and 34.

Sites 6–8 are right along the edge of the lake, affording a commanding view of the water and beyond—and totally exposed to anyone driving by on this short spur that heads to the boat ramp. These sites do not offer any sense of privacy. Site 9 is at the north end of the spur and separated slightly from site 8. It's next to the trail to the fishing pier and right off a small parking area. Of all the sites in the campground, these are last resorts, in my opinion.

Saving the best for last, I highly recommend any of the walk-in sites, especially if you like roughing it at a very basic campsite right at the water's edge. The best of these is site 5, at the southern end of a Y-shaped trail spur, about 100 yards from the parking area. It may get noisy at the nearby boat launch, but these are still premium spots for purist campers. Main activity offerings include fishing, swimming, boating, and hiking.

Crescent Lake Campground

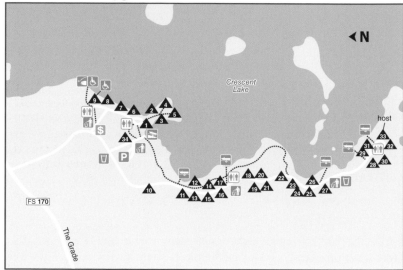

GETTING THERE

From the intersection of MN 61 and Sawbill Trail/CR 2 in Tofte, head north on Sawbill Trail/CR 2. Go about 17 miles to the CRESCENT LAKE sign to FS 170/The Grade (many maps note this as FS 165). Go right (east) 6.8 miles to the campground road on the right.

GPS COORDINATES: N47° 50.066′ W90° 46.291′

6

Devil Track Lake Campground

Beauty ★★★ / Privacy ★★★★★ / Spaciousness ★★★★★ / Quiet ★★★★ / Security ★★★★ / Cleanliness ★★★

The closest campground to Grand Marais, Devil Track is situated on a peninsula at the western end of a long, narrow lake.

When you drive into Devil Track Lake Campground, you might do a double take upon seeing the size of many of the campsites; they are huge expanses of grass. You could arrive in a bus and put up a circus tent and still have room for more. These sites are incredibly spacious—and therefore private.

Being as close as it is to Grand Marais, the lake serves two masters: those who want the amenities of a recreational water playground (motorboating, sailing, and even floatplanes) and those who want to feel that the north woods is right in the backyard. The campground is laid out along on a broad, knobby peninsula near the western end of the lake.

I was dumbfounded when I drove into the site I had selected: The driveway extended nearly 50 yards long before coming to a Y intersection. My site was 4, to the left. That spur seemed to go on forever, too, before it came to the campsite itself. A broad, dense understory of mixed aspen and balsam fir separated my camp from site 3. Another line of trees separated the site from the lake. The rest of the area was a large, lawn-covered field that could easily allow me to pitch several more tents. The lone picnic table and fire ring are almost lost within the expansive site.

Sunset on Devil Track Lake

courtesy of Skyport Lodge on Devil Track Lake

KEY INFORMATION

ADDRESS: Forest Route 1612, 0.2 mile south of Devil Track Road, Grand Marais, MN 55604

CONTACT: 218-387-1750, tinyurl.com /deviltracklakecg

OPERATED BY: Superior National Forest, Gunflint Ranger District

OPEN: Year-round, when accessible (facilities: early May–mid-October; no fees or services in winter)

SITES: 16 rustic; group sites available

EACH SITE HAS: Open tent area, picnic table, fire ring (premium sites available)

WHEELCHAIR ACCESS: No designated sites

ASSIGNMENT: First come, first served (no reservations)

REGISTRATION: Fee station at campground entrance

FACILITIES: Vault toilet, water

PARKING: 1 vehicle/site; half fee/additional vehicle at site (must park on spur)

FEES: $16/night, $18/night premium sites

RESTRICTIONS:

PETS: Under owner's control at all times

QUIET HOURS: 10 p.m.–6 a.m.

FIRES: In fire rings; gathering of downed or dead firewood permitted; firewood must be purchased from approved vendor; non-ash firewood gathered within 100 miles of Superior National Forest permitted

ALCOHOL: Permitted

OTHER: 9 people/site; use the facilities provided, such as tent pads and latrines; dispose of garbage in containers provided; water faucets for collecting water only—do not use area to wash dishes, fish, or other items; noise limits enforced at developed sites

The campground is basically a long, curving stretch of camping spots along the lake with only four sites on the other side of the road. The road forms a cul-de-sac at the far end and makes a loop, with a lone site on it halfway back to the entrance. The area has mostly younger trees—aspen and spruce, with an occasional red pine and a few birch clumps scattered throughout the woods.

Site 1 is at the end of a 100-foot driveway and opens up into an immense area. The site is off to the right of a clearing where campers can get drinking water. Site 2 sits amid a stand of aspen saplings. Sites 3 and 4 are at the end of a long Y-shaped driveway, each at one end of the upper arms of the Y. These are the first sites that sit right on the lake; it's only about 10 feet to the water from these big sites! Likewise, site 5 is large, with a long drive drawing you into the trees. Ditto for site 6, also flanked by young aspens.

Sites 7 and 8 are on a broad plateau—not as big as the others, but ample and situated right above the lake's edge. Site 9 is at the end of the driveway that makes a beeline shot back to the campground. There is what seems to be a pull-through drive off the road at site 10. It's handy because it's blocked at one end; it best serves as a place to park your vehicle so it can at least partially block the view from the road.

Sites 12 and 14 are actually standard-size lots. Site 13 is a small site right on the road. Fortunately there is a small clump of birches serving as a visual screen for this site. The last site at the end of the road before the cul-de-sac is 15, a basic, "small" site when compared to the megasites here. Site 16 is off by itself on the back side of the loop that encircles the entrance.

Devil Track Lake would be the perfect place for a family that enjoys playing yard games while camping—there's ample room to set up several different games at the same time. Of course, the lake is great for canoeing or kayaking; access at some sites is down a grassy or earthen embankment with a few boulders. There is a major floatplane base just east of the campground. Floatplane operations could provide entertainment, or some unwelcome noise.

Another nice treat about these sites is the openness to the sky—this would be an ideal campground for gazing at the Milky Way, summer meteor showers, and the occasional display of the northern lights. Main activities include fishing, swimming, and boating.

Devil Track Lake Campground

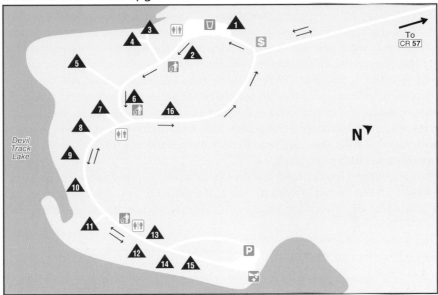

GETTING THERE

From Grand Marais take Gunflint Trail/CR 12 north 4 miles to Devil Track Road/CR 8. Turn left (west), and go 5.6 miles to the junction with CR 57. Stay left and go 2.7 miles, then turn left onto FS 1612. Go 0.2 mile to the campground.

GPS COORDINATES: N47° 49.808 W90° 28.019'

7

Fenske Lake Campground

Beauty ★★★ / Privacy ★★★★★ / Spaciousness ★★★ / Quiet ★★★ / Security ★★★★ / Cleanliness ★★★

Here you'll find remote camping under an impressive stand of old-growth pines, next to a northern lake and the Echo Trail.

Note: As of March 2018, this campground was still a work in progress after the devastating storm of July 2016, in which many trees were uprooted or otherwise destroyed. The campground is still in some disarray but is being cleaned and groomed as quickly as possible.

By the time you've driven into Ely, the spirit of all that is northern Minnesota surrounds you. This is Boundary Waters Canoe Area Wilderness (BWCAW) country. Up the famous Echo Trail, every turn brings you closer to the remoteness and beauty of this country. Entering the campground at Fenske Lake brings it all home as the road climbs up a ridge guarded by stately white pines with a solid understory of balsam firs and old-growth aspens. As the road continues to the campground, the forest expands to include jack pines mixed with paper birch.

The campground is an elongated loop of 15 campsites perched above Fenske Lake. Site 1 is very small and immediately to the left of the driveway into site 2 with its incredibly long, white pine–lined corridor. Site 2 sits completely alone on the slopes of this section

Fenske Lake from the boat launch area

KEY INFORMATION

ADDRESS: 2229 Echo Trail, Ely, MN 55731

CONTACT: Concessionaire: 218-365-2963, camprrm.com/parks/fenske-lake-campground; Kawishiwi Ranger District: 218-235-1299, tinyurl.com/fenskelakecg

OPERATED BY: Superior National Forest, Kawishiwi Ranger District (operated by Recreation Resource Management)

OPEN: Year-round (facilities: Mid-May–September; no fees or services in winter)

SITES: 14, 1 walk-in, 1 group

EACH SITE HAS: Open tent area, picnic table, fire ring

WHEELCHAIR ACCESS: Site 14 and group site

ASSIGNMENT: Both open and reserved

REGISTRATION: Fee station at entrance; reserve at 877-444-6777 or recreation.gov

FACILITIES: Vault toilet, water, Dumpster, pavilion, wheelchair-accessible facilities

PARKING: 1 vehicle/site; at trailhead to walk-in site; half fee/additional vehicle at site (must park on spur); also at boat ramp and pavilion

FEES: $15/night

RESTRICTIONS:

PETS: Under owner's control at all times

QUIET HOURS: 10 p.m.–6 a.m.

FIRES: In fire rings; gathering of downed or dead firewood permitted; firewood must be purchased from approved vendor; non-ash firewood gathered within 100 miles of Superior National Forest permitted

ALCOHOL: Permitted

OTHER: 9 people/site; noise limits enforced at developed sites

of the ridge. Site 3, under the cover of mature white and red pine, is spacious, with an open understory back off the road as well. The campground road is still climbing the ridge at site 4, a nondescript site. Small site 5, however, marks the top of the ridge and is laid out under a stand of stately pines. Site 6 is also small—a mini walk-in with parking off the road and a short trail leading to what looks to be a picnic site with a tent space. Both 5 and 6 are on the outside of the loop, backed by the pine forest. Every site is spread far apart, so privacy is maximized at Fenske Lake—especially at sites along the back side of the loop away from the lake.

Site 7 is the odd (but beautiful) duck at this campground because it's really a walk-in site situated right on the shore of the lake. A parking space right off the road, between sites 6 and 7, marks the trail to site 7. The trail drops down through the trees to the water's edge. If you have the energy to haul your stuff down the ridge and back, this is the site worth staking out.

Site 8 is another drop-off campsite—literally. It drops down from the roadway to a level campsite overlooking the lake (through the trees). Site 9 (wheelchair accessible) is an inside-the-loop site that sits back from the road. It backs up to site 4, but there are plenty of trees and distance to keep it secluded as well.

Site 10 sits perched halfway between the roadway and the lake, on a plateau on the side of the ridge. Likewise for site 11, except it is slightly more exposed than its neighbor. Sites 12 and 13 have these plateau or shelf areas as well. All look down toward the lake and drop down from the road slightly. These sites offer less privacy than those mentioned earlier. There is a paved, 750-foot access trail to the lake that runs from the pavilion across the road and winds its way down the ridge below site 13—at up to a 5.5% grade. It swings past the picnic area and ends at the fishing pier at the lake.

There's also a trail that begins at the parking area at the pavilion and circles around almost the entire campground (site 7 is located adjacent to this trail). It intersects with a short path between sites 12 and 13, enabling hikers to go back up to the pavilion or continue down to the lake at the swimming beach.

Sites 14 and 15 almost make a combination site because they are each on short spurs that come off a Y driveway. Site 15 is right next door—seemingly an arm's length away. Site 14 is wheelchair accessible.

Fenske Lake's group site (wheelchair-accessible site 16) is noteworthy. It is located a few hundred yards farther up the Echo Trail (just past the entrance to the Fenske Lake boat landing area). This campsite sits atop the ridge, under majestic white and red pines. There are two very spacious areas overlooking the lake.

Fenske Lake looks the part of a BWCAW lake: it has the rocky, boulder-strewn shoreline and the islands and outcrops of the exposed Canadian Shield bedrock, and it has been graced with a full forest of red and white pines. Campgrounds closer to BWCAW access points may get crowded during the summer. Fenske Lake and other forest campgrounds can provide the perfect alternative for your camping outing. It's also the perfect lake to perhaps avoid the BWCAW area for a weekend of swimming, canoeing, or fishing.

Fenske Lake Campground

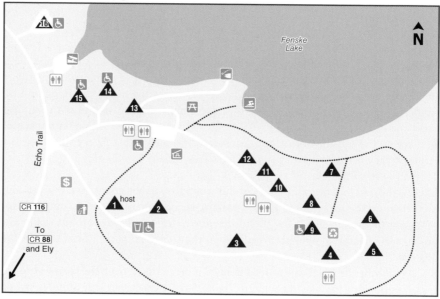

GETTING THERE

From Ely go 1 mile east on MN 169 to CR 88. Turn left (north) and go 2 miles to Echo Trail (CR 116). Turn right (north) and go 7.6 miles to the campground entrance on the right.

GPS COORDINATES: N47° 59.792' W91° 55.057'

8

Flour Lake Campground

Beauty ★★★★ / Privacy ★★★★ / Spaciousness ★★★★ / Quiet ★★★★ / Security ★★★ / Cleanliness ★★★★

All the charm of a north-woods lake, on the very edge of the Boundary Waters

Flour Lake is one of those gems in the Superior National Forest's jewel box of campgrounds. It is situated right at the edge of the Boundary Waters Canoe Area Wilderness (BWCAW)—literally, as its east end is an entry point (don't forget your permit if you will be overnighting in the BWCAW; overnight permits are $16/person plus $10 reservation fee; self-issued day-use permits are free).

Flour Lake is a 3.5-mile-by-0.5-mile pristine body of water with clarity to more than 20 feet and a maximum depth of more than 100 feet. Towering white and red pines and paper birches with white curly bark line the shores. Anglers know the lake for its walleye, lake trout, northern pike, and smallmouth bass.

The campgrounds are laid out in an elongated loop offering spacious campsites. Site 1 (wheelchair accessible) is immediately behind the registration kiosk, so be prepared for some late-night activity as guests register. The site is flat and lined with a variety of trees. Site 2 is long and narrow and backs up and into site 30. Site 3—a fairly private site—is small and slopes down slightly away from the road. Site 4 is long and narrow, stretching straight back through a dense understory.

Site 5 is a short spur with a cozy tent spot close to the road. Site 6 is a long, dogleg-shaped site with a slight uphill incline. Site 7 is expansive compared to the others so far. It has room for two to three tents and is flanked by a stately red pine and a mature paper birch.

Site 8 (wheelchair accessible) is long and narrow with space back off the road, ranking it high on the privacy meter. At site 9 you can park to the left of the driveway and pitch your

Canoeing Flour Lake on the edge of the Boundary Waters Canoe Area Wilderness

KEY INFORMATION

ADDRESS: 1 mile south of concessionaire adjacent to campground: Golden Eagle Lodge Inc., 468 Clearwater Road/CR 22, Grand Marais, MN 55604

CONTACT: Gunflint Ranger District: 218-387-1750, tinyurl.com/flourlakecg; Golden Eagle Lodge: 218-388–2203, golden-eagle.com

OPERATED BY: Superior National Forest, Gunflint Ranger District

OPEN: Year-round (usually accessible mid-May–mid-October; no fees or services in winter)

SITES: 37

EACH SITE HAS: Open tent area, picnic table, fire ring

WHEELCHAIR ACCESS: Sites 1, 8, 21, 23, and 34

ASSIGNMENT: 27 reservable; 10 first come, first served

REGISTRATION: Reserve at 877-444-6777 or recreation.gov

FACILITIES: Drinking water, vault toilet, boat launch

PARKING: 1 vehicle/site; $10/additional vehicle (must park on spur); also at boat ramp and in cul-de-sac for sites 18 and 19

FEES: $20/night

RESTRICTIONS:

PETS: On leash

QUIET HOURS: 10 p.m.–6 a.m.

FIRES: In fire rings; gathering of downed or dead firewood permitted; firewood must be purchased from approved vendor; non-ash firewood gathered within 100 miles of Superior National Forest permitted

ALCOHOL: Responsible use permitted

OTHER: 9 people/site; 14-day stay limit

tent on the other side. Site 10 is an elongated site surrounded by a mature stand of trees—nice! Site 11 is a flattened Y shape with lots of room to set up your tent(s).

Site 12 is spacious, while 13 has one good spot but has an open view from the road. Site 14 has space for a few tents down a campsite that's long and narrow but not level enough to enjoy a comfortable sleep. Site 15 is T-shaped with a spacious section off to the right. Site 16 is long and straight, very open and easily viewable from the road. Site 17 sits back in the trees from the road and is surrounded by lush forest.

Site 18 is one of my favorites in Minnesota. It's on a circular spur off the main campground road and is accessible by a short incline from the parking area. You can't see a lot of the lake from this site, which is perched on a ridge running parallel to the shore, but the wide-open yet tree-lined site can easily hold two to three tents. One tent site is a small knob facing the lake—an ideal location.

Site 19 runs a close second as a choice location to camp. It is accessible by a short walk through a tree-lined corridor that opens onto a small clearing surrounded by trees and understory so thick you cannot see the lake 40 yards down the slope. It is a wonderful site and the most private in the campground.

Site 20 features a short driveway leading to a long, L-shaped campsite. Site 21 (wheelchair accessible) is a broad site with stately spruce and birch trees accenting the landscape. Site 22 is a large site well suited for an RV or trailer. Site 23 (wheelchair accessible) is equally huge, a spacious site with tall, mature trees.

Site 24 has space and privacy and would make a good group site. Site 25 reflects the diversity of trees that thrive here. This T-shaped campsite has a small stand of cedars and room for several tents.

Sites 26–37 vary slightly in layout, but each offers plenty of room to pitch a tent—or two, or even more in the case of sites 27 and 30. Site 27 has a short driveway and several spaces cut into a long campsite. Several tents could be pitched in its little alcove of trees. Site 28 is very open—not a lot of shade. Site 29 has a T-shaped camping area with two tent areas. Site 30 is incredibly long (site 2 extends into it) with two picnic tables and two fire rings. Site 31 is laid out behind a small island of shrubbery that screens it from the road, making it one of the more private sites in the loop. Site 32 is long, narrow, and one of the shadier sites. Site 33 is average, while site 34 (wheelchair accessible) is long, deep, and flanked on one side by fir trees.

Just up the road from the campground entrance is the start of a short hike and easy stairway climb that leads to Honeymoon Bluff, overlooking Hungry Jack Lake to the north. A 9-mile trail around Flour Lake takes hikers to virgin white pines. Overlooks abound. If you head back out to the Gunflint Trail and go north a few miles to the Trail Center Restaurant, you'll find the best rib-sticking food in this part of the north country.

Since you're already halfway up the Gunflint Trail, consider your next campsite at Trail's End. It's at the far end of the trail and features short, walk-in campsites at the edge of the northernmost sections of the BWCAW. It's a popular entry point for the Sea Gull and Saganaga Lake systems. The campground features awesome rocky landscapes and incredible vistas in a classic north-country campsite setting.

Flour Lake Campground

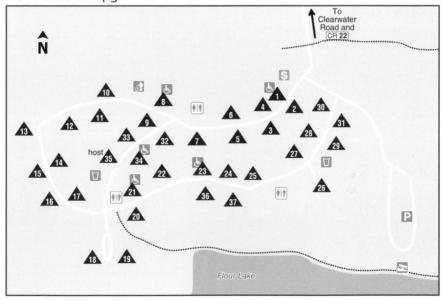

GETTING THERE

From MN 61 in Grand Marais go north on CR 12 (the Gunflint Trail) 27.3 miles to Clearwater Road/CR 22 (some maps may indicate this as CR 66). Turn east (right) and go 2.1 miles to the entrance to the campground on the right.

GPS COORDINATES: N48° 3.188' W90° 24.421'

9

Hayes Lake State Park Campground

Beauty ★★ / Privacy ★★★ / Spaciousness ★★★ / Quiet ★★★ / Security ★★★ / Cleanliness ★★★★

This isolated camping hideaway on a lake and stream is tucked in the middle of a state forest.

Hayes Lake is one of very few places to camp in the extreme northwestern corner of Minnesota. It's not even on many pass-through routes—you have to want to come here. That said, this campground would be a typical one in the more heavily used areas of the state. In this region, with the Canadian border peeking out at the northern horizon, it's a quaint, homey spot in a pleasant, classic northern Minnesota setting.

Situated on a man-made lake created when the north fork of the Roseau River was dammed, Hayes Lake is surrounded by hundreds of square miles of Minnesota "wilderness" protected in the Beltrami Island State Forest. The park is noted for its scenery and solitude—the former being especially welcome in this sparse, flat area. The prehistoric glacial Lake Agassiz played a major role in shaping the landscape. The flat topography, with its poor drainage, created numerous bogs throughout the low-lying areas. Muskegs created healthy environments for a variety of wildlife. If you're seeking a chance

Hayes Lake and shoreline

KEY INFORMATION

ADDRESS: 48990 CR 4, Roseau, MN 56751
(park entrance is 0.8 mile east)

CONTACT: 218-425-7504, dnr.state.mn.us
/state_parks/hayes_lake

OPERATED BY: Minnesota DNR, Division of
Parks and Recreation

OPEN: Early May–late October (facilities:
mid-May–September)

SITES: 35 (18 with electric), 2 walk-in,
2 camper cabins

EACH SITE HAS: Open tent area, picnic
table, fire ring

WHEELCHAIR ACCESS: Site 20

ASSIGNMENT: Reservations required
(same-day reservations available)

REGISTRATION: Reserve at 866-85-PARKS
(72757) or tinyurl.com/mnspreservations

FACILITIES: Restrooms, showers, vault toilets,
water, RV sanitation station, boat launch

PARKING: 1 vehicle/site

FEES: $15/night, $23/night electric sites,
$7 daily permit, $35 annual permit, $8.50
reservation fee

RESTRICTIONS:

PETS: On 6-foot leash; attended at all times

QUIET HOURS: 10 p.m.–8 a.m.

FIRES: In fire rings; gathering firewood not
permitted; firewood must be purchased
from approved vendor

ALCOHOL: Not permitted

OTHER: 6 people/site; closed to visitors
10 p.m.–8 a.m.; fireworks and metal detectors prohibited; only electric motors on lake

encounter with a bear, moose, fisher, otter, bobcat, lynx, or timber wolf, Hayes Lake is the site to place your bets.

This area was homesteaded in the early 1900s. The Homestead Trail offers glimpses into the region's historic, natural, and cultural past.

The main campground is located halfway through the park, on the northern side of the lake. Thirty-five campsites are placed along two elongated loops. The first loop (loop A) contains 26 sites with scrubby understory and grass, resulting in little privacy. Wheelchair-accessible site 20 is located in this loop. Sites are rather close together for my liking but are typical of most Department of Natural Resources sites. The campsites are staggered and not that far from the lake. Although they are not right near the lakeshore, sites 22 and 23 are the ones I'd head for first.

Loop B features sites 27–35, all of which are surrounded by a stand of young tamarack and spruce. These sites tend to be long, narrow, and covered with grass. Both loops are close to the Bog Walk, a wooden walkway that winds through a wetlands bog area.

The Bog Walk links up about 0.125 mile from the end of the campsite loops. Insect repellent and a bug screen are recommended. As a nature trail, the Bog Walk excels. Orchids and other unique bog plants can be observed right from the walkway. Boardwalkers can bird-watch and view wildlife or just enjoy sitting on one of the many benches along this interpretive trail. The entire wetlands area, from the serpentine shoreline of Hayes Lake to the many creeks of the Little Roseau River, creates a finite ecosystem of special value—especially in these far reaches of Minnesota.

The Pine Ridge Trail offers interpretive signs and follows the entire campground side of the lake, and several side loops head off from this main trail to create a network of trails throughout the park.

The park borders sections of the Red Lake Indian Reservation, and there are numerous private properties as well, so it's important and respectful to stay on the designated trails.

For the family wanting a remote, far-northern-country experience away from the madding—or any—crowd, Hayes Lake may be perfect. For the loner or a small group of campers, Hayes Lake may be the answer to the quest for solitude. Old Mill State Park and Lake Bronson State Park lie about 50 miles west as the crow flies and offer pleasant campgrounds when in this region of extreme northwest Minnesota.

Hayes Lake State Park Campground

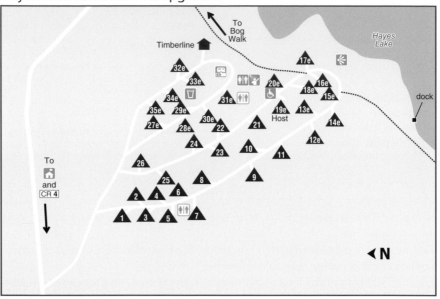

GETTING THERE

From Roseau take MN 89 south 15 miles through Wannaska to CR 4. Turn left (east) on CR 4 and go almost 9 miles to the park entrance on the right (River Forest Road).

GPS COORDINATES: N48° 38.047' W95° 32.206'

10

Huntersville Forest and Shell City Campgrounds

Beauty ★★★ / Privacy ★★★ / Spaciousness ★★★ / Quiet ★★★ / Security ★★★ / Cleanliness ★★★

Quaint and somewhat Spartan campsites—each on the banks of small, northern forest rivers—just a short drive from Lake Itasca.

This is a twofer because Huntersville Forest and Shell City Campgrounds provide a similar camping experience. They are both in the same state forest, on small rivers ideal for fishing and canoeing, and are modest in their facilities. They are only a short distance from Itasca State Park, meaning they offer a more modest, yet adequate, alternative to the campgrounds at the bigger state park complex. In fact, they are managed by Itasca State Park, so they may be referral sites for overflow camping.

Huntersville State Forest comprises 52 square miles of mostly red and jack pine forests with a scattering of aspen and spruce and a variety of northern hardwood covering rolling, sandy hills. The area is cut by two rivers, the Crow Wing and the Shell. Like most of Minnesota's state forests, this one is managed for its forest resources but provides some recreational opportunities. Campsites are typically at water's edge—the main activities are usually boating and fishing.

Along the banks of Crow Wing River, one of Minnesota's designated water trails

KEY INFORMATION

ADDRESS: Huntersville: 35550 Campsite Drive, Menahga, MN 56464; Shell City: 390th Street, 0.5 mile east of 199th Avenue/CR 24, Menahga, MN 56464

CONTACT: 218-699-7251, dnr.state.mn.us /state_forests/facilities/cmp00028 and dnr.state.mn.us/state_forests/facilities /cmp00027

OPERATED BY: Minnesota DNR, Division of Forestry (managed by Itasca State Park)

OPEN: April–December, when accessible

SITES: Huntersville Forest: 24, 5 walk-in, 2 group; Shell City: 19, 8 equestrian

EACH SITE HAS: Open tent area, picnic table, fire ring

WHEELCHAIR ACCESS: No designated sites

ASSIGNMENT: First come, first served

REGISTRATION: Fee/registration station at each campground

FACILITIES: Vault toilets, well water, boat ramp at Huntersville (carry-in access at Shell City)

PARKING: 1 vehicle/site (2 vehicles/site with permission); at trailheads to walk-in sites; at boat ramp (Huntersville)

FEES: $14/night

RESTRICTIONS:

PETS: On leash only

QUIET HOURS: 10 p.m.–8 a.m.

FIRES: In fire rings; gathering downed and dead firewood permitted; firewood must be purchased from approved vendor

ALCOHOL: Not permitted

OTHER: 8 people/site; hunting and firearms only in posted areas; camping possible in undeveloped areas (special rules apply)

The Shell City Campground is adjacent to a horse camp whose campers can use 22 miles of horse trails. In the winter, snowmobilers race along 15 miles of dedicated trails. Hikers should find plenty of places to trek using the 150-plus miles of logging trails throughout the forest. These routes are shared by hikers, bikers, and drivers.

The big attraction at these two campgrounds is the river flowing past each. Both the Shell and the Crow Wing Rivers (one of Minnesota's State Water Trails) provide many canoeing opportunities, with access ramps at the campgrounds, as well as other put-in and take-out points along the river's course through the forest. These are accessed by landing turnouts along county roads in the area. This boating route winds along 80 miles of river and offers a wilderness campsite every 3–7 miles. The Shell flows into the Crow Wing a few miles east of the Shell City Campground.

The campground at Huntersville looks more like a picnic area with tent sites. The best camping is at the group sites, which ensure a spacious site and a better chance at a more private experience. These sites are set in a dense stand of aspen, birch, and maple. Because a large family with at least two or three tents—or a group of friends with as many or more—qualifies as a group, these are definitely the sites to claim. Of the two sites, D4 and D5 are more open and spacious.

The sites at Shell City are more wooded. The Shell River is a slow-moving, peaceful stream with lush reeds and rushes growing along its banks. Like the Crow Wing, it is a relatively shallow, sandy-bottomed river (good for swimming) that meanders peacefully through stands of pine. The campground itself is under a towering stand of white pine and close to the road. It's not overly private, but the mood is certainly inviting.

The state forests are managed for their timber, and the recreational amenities are usually minimal unless your camping weekend revolves around boating and fishing—or you are

able to entertain yourself without programs and interpretive trails. The independent birder/
photographer/wildlife viewer will be right at home in these modest campgrounds. If that
sounds like you, these two campgrounds are ideal for a casual, low-key weekend or longer
camping experience. The self-sufficient canoe camper will enjoy the paddling routes while
the hiker explores all the logging roads.

A word of warning: All the roads in the state forest are open to all-terrain vehicles during
the summer months. Be advised, too, that many of the state forest campgrounds are used by
horseback riders, for either camping or day use. Trails used by horses tend to get churned up
into a fine dust or excessively mired in the rain. Check the campground map—most trails are
designated, so be sure to stay off the horse trails and hope riders do likewise with the hiking-
only routes. Other activities include snowmobiling, hiking trails, swimming, and boating.

Huntersville Forest and Shell City Campgrounds

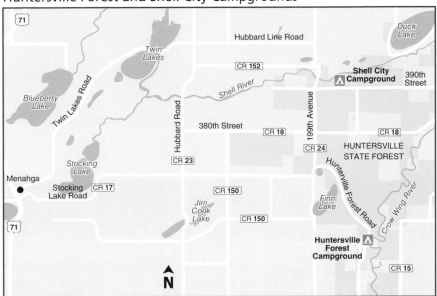

GETTING THERE

Huntersville: From Menahga take Stocking Lake Road east 4 miles to CR 23 (Hubbard
Road), turn left (north), and go 1 mile to 380th Street (CR 18). Turn right (east) and travel
3 miles to 199th Avenue (CR 24); turn right (south), go 1 mile to the sign, turn left, and go
about 2 miles.

Shell City: From Menahga take Stocking Lake Road east 4 miles to CR 23, turn left,
and go 1 mile to 380th Street. Turn right and go 3 miles to 199th Avenue; turn left (north)
and go 0.5 mile. Turn right (east) on to 390th Street. The entrance to Shell City Campground is about 0.5 mile on left.

GPS COORDINATES:
HUNTERSVILLE FOREST: N46° 44.295' W94° 55.770'
SHELL CITY: N46° 47.420' W94° 56.524'

11

Indian Lake Campground

Beauty ★★★★ / Privacy ★★★ / Spaciousness ★★★★ / Quiet ★★★★ / Security ★★★★ / Cleanliness ★★★★

Roomy campsites situated beneath red pines offer access to a small, northern lake.

Indian Lake features two campground loops, both close to the lake and each with fairly large, open campsites that offer plenty of room to spread out and enjoy the scattered forest of red and white pines, spruces, and aspens. Both loops provide easy access to the main campground trail that goes along the lake.

Loop B has 18 campsites along a spur off the road leading to the boat ramp. Sites 1 and 2 are large, grassy areas separated by a row of caragana hedging planted as a natural fence between the sites. These long sites have plenty of room for tents—but will probably be snatched up by RVs because of the long driveways. The same can be said about sites 3–6. Site 7 has a view of the lake beyond its boundaries. Otherwise it is typical of the remaining sites within this loop.

Trails lead to the beach area from the main road in loop B. These are located across the road from the access driveways to sites 6, 8, and 11.

Site 11 has its own appeal because it's back in a corner by itself—creating a private retreat away from the rest in the loop. Sites 12 and 13 are off toward the water, but both are

Campsite in a stand of red pines

KEY INFORMATION

ADDRESS: Brimson Road/CR 44, 1.2 miles north of Two Harbors-Brimson Road, Brimson, MN 55602

CONTACT: 218-595-7625, dnr.state.mn.us /state_forests/facilities/cmp00009

OPERATED BY: Cloquet Valley State Forest (managed by Split Rock Lighthouse State Park)

OPEN: Year-round, when accessible (facilities: mid-May–mid-October)

SITES: 20, 5 walk-in

EACH SITE HAS: Open tent area, picnic table, fire ring

WHEELCHAIR ACCESS: Site 17

ASSIGNMENT: First come, first served

REGISTRATION: No reservations, except for group site (check with Split Rock Lighthouse State Park for details)

FACILITIES: Vault toilets, water

PARKING: 2 vehicles/site (additional vehicles with permission); at trailheads to walk-in sites; also at picnic area and boat ramp

FEES: $14/night; group site $50/night or $3/person, whichever is greater

---

RESTRICTIONS:

PETS: On leash

QUIET HOURS: 10 p.m.–8 a.m.

FIRES: In fire rings; gathering of downed or dead firewood permitted; firewood must be purchased from approved vendor

ALCOHOL: Not permitted

OTHER: 8 people/site; firearms only in posted areas; camping possible in undeveloped areas (special rules apply)

nondescript and basic. These three campsites are situated along a spur that leads down to the boat access and fishing pier. Site 11 is situated at the end of a long driveway, making it a narrow site that parallels the road down to the lake. Site 12 is open and flat with a nice view of the lake. A very exposed campsite with a small, slightly sloping tent site makes site 13 questionable unless you consider the gorgeous view it provides from its perch overlooking the water. Sitting on a knoll above the lake, this site is also one of the most picturesque in the park. Site 14 (part of the loop again) and 15 are both open, with no privacy from the road. Site 16 is not particularly noteworthy, and 17 is the wheelchair-accessible site. All these sites at the bottom of loop B are close to the road—not too appealing.

The second loop at Indian Lake features sites labeled walk-ins merely because you have to park your vehicle at a turnout and walk down to them—maybe 20 or 30 yards, tops. This jaunt through the forest will reward you with expansive sites (in view of one another—the only downside to them) under tall red pines and amid full-bodied spruce trees.

In this same loop are two drive-up sites, 19 and 20. These are in a stand of red and white pines—almost a plantation planting; the red pines align to form a corridor as you enter this loop. This area is nicely laid out, with alders and dogwoods creating a lush understory. The loop is set along a ridge or rise above the lake. Site 19 features a tent pad on a flat area above the lake (in the distance). Site 20 is slightly smaller, backed by the woods, and very private—except for the fact that it is right across from 19.

Sites 21–25 are the walk-in sites. Sites 21 and 22 are off into the woods toward the lake. Site 22 is more open and grassy and a bit farther from the road. Site 23 is a very short distance from the turnout parking area, while 24 has a true walk-in feel to it. Once back in the camping areas, however, sites open up to reveal themselves to one another. Campers in any of these sites can look through a sparse planting of smaller trees to see neighboring sites—limited privacy from one another, even though they are quite private from the campground loop road. This may not be a bad thing if larger groups—a family reunion or gathering—want to camp together but still maintain some privacy immediately around their own tent sites.

Site 25 is open and very spacious but, again, within view of other sites. These sites are further screened by balsam firs, so there are some visual buffers throughout this otherwise open area.

All in all, these walk-in sites are large, spacious, grassy areas in which to enjoy the modest lake. These sites require that you carry your gear a short distance. There is ample parking for small groups sharing a site or two.

A trail along the lakeshore is accessible from all the sites in loop B. There is also a trail leading from site 23 to the water pump and then on to the beach area.

Indian Lake is a shallow lake on the Cloquet River State Water Trail, making this a great stopover campground or put-in/take-out spot on a weekend paddling adventure. In any case, camping at Indian Lake offers the basics in north-woods settings with a typical—clean, spacious—state forest campground experience. Other activities include swimming, canoeing, and fishing.

Indian Lake Campground

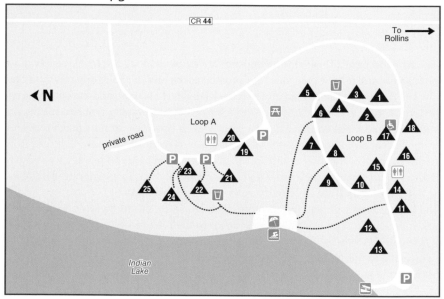

GETTING THERE

From Two Harbors take CR 2 north 13 miles to CR 14. Turn left (west) and go 12 miles to Rollins. Turn right (north) onto CR 44 and drive 1.25 miles to the campground entrance on the left.

GPS COORDINATES: N47° 16.435' W91° 50.757'

12

⚠ Itasca State Park and Hungryman Forest Campgrounds

Beauty ★★★★ / Privacy ★★★ / Spaciousness ★★ / Quiet ★★ / Security ★★★ / Cleanliness ★★★

This showcase, pine-forested park features the source of the Mississippi River.

There are two things all elementary school students in Minnesota know by heart: that their state is the land of 10,000 lakes and that Lake Itasca is the birthplace of the mighty Mississippi River. Naturally, the park bearing that name attracts tourists who come to enjoy its natural attractions—and often to camp. With more than 32,000 acres within its boundaries, scores of lakes, and more than 50 miles of hiking trails, Lake Itasca pleases visitors with ease. All that and more await under majestic northern red-pine forests.

There is nothing more tranquil than boating on a Minnesota lake at sunset. The long, narrow arms of Itasca offer miles of canoeing opportunities. You can paddle from the North Arm boat ramp a thousand yards farther north and come to a small creek flowing gently out of the lake. Pass through the boulders across this flow and keep heading downstream. A few thousand miles later, you'll be paddling in the Gulf of Mexico.

Launch from that same boat ramp and head in the opposite direction, and you'll reach the end of the East Arm, where the grandness of Douglas Lodge looms overhead. Step ashore and you are in the heart of the most developed part of this large park. From here you can take several main trails to lakes and points south, or you can hop in a car (or on a bike) and enjoy 10 miles of pure northern Minnesota near-wilderness as you wind along the perimeter of the Itasca Wilderness Sanctuary Scientific and Natural Area.

Itasca's biggest attraction: the headwaters of the Mississippi River

KEY INFORMATION

ADDRESS: Itasca State Park: 36750 Main Park Drive, Park Rapids, MN 56470 (continue 2.4 miles to Campground Road for both campgrounds); Hungryman Forest: Becker Line Road, 0.5 mile north of CR 41, Park Rapids, MN 56470

CONTACT: 218-699-7251, dnr.state.mn.us /state_parks/itasca; dnr.state.mn.us/state _forests/facilities/cmp00048

OPERATED BY: Minnesota DNR, Division of Parks and Recreation (Hungryman Forest: managed by Itasca State Park)

OPEN: Mid-May–early October (limited sites year-round at Pine Ridge)

SITES: Itasca State Park: 223 (160 with electric), 11 cart-in, 11 backpack-in, 6 camper cabins, 1 guesthouse, 1 group; Hungryman Forest: 14

EACH SITE HAS: Open tent area, picnic table, fire ring

WHEELCHAIR ACCESS: Sites 155 and 156 in Pine Ridge and sites 19 and 21 in Bear Paw

ASSIGNMENT: Itasca State Park: Reservations required (same-day reservations available); Hungryman Forest: First come, first served

REGISTRATION: Reserve at 866-85-PARKS (72757) or tinyurl.com/mnspreservations

FACILITIES: Itasca State Park: Restrooms, showers, vault toilets, water, RV sanitation station; Hungryman: Water, vault toilets

PARKING: 1 vehicle/site; parking area at each loop; at trailhead to cart-in sites

FEES: $23/night, $17 off-season, $31/night electric sites, $7 daily permit, $35 annual permit, $8.50 reservation fee

---

RESTRICTIONS:

PETS: On 6-foot leash; attended at all times

QUIET HOURS: 10 p.m.–8 a.m.

FIRES: In fire rings; gathering firewood not permitted; firewood must be purchased from approved vendor

ALCOHOL: Not permitted

OTHER: 6 people/site; closed to visitors 10 p.m.–8 a.m.; fireworks and metal detectors prohibited

---

As a student at the University of Minnesota's College of Forestry back in the late 1960s, I spent five weeks at Lake Itasca during a field semester. We saw the campgrounds every day during that late-summer session. They were always full, and the tents were all concentrated in two rather confined areas in this expansive park. I've camped there a few times since my college days, and when I went back there again to inspect the grounds for this chapter, I found that the campgrounds at Itasca are still pretty average; the trees are bigger, the understory thicker, and the campgrounds filled with campers.

The sites are cozy, set under stands of pine or the more common aspen, especially at the Pine Ridge site. They are basic Department of Natural Resources campsites: driveway, picnic table, and fire ring. Bear Paw is at least near the lake, but it is also the preferred site for the big RV units. Pine Ridge is within modest walking distance to the lake and a strip of amenities along the shore, from boat ramp to swimming beach to amphitheater.

Camping at Itasca is convenient for enjoying all the other natural amenities of this park. You probably aren't going to spend a lot of time sitting around your tent—there's too much to do and too many places to see on foot or with wheels of one type or another. There are several walk-in and primitive campsites throughout the park as well.

Itasca offers myriad recreational activities, including fishing (and rod and reel rentals); swimming; canoe, kayak, pontoon, boat, and stand-up paddleboard rentals; biking (and bike rentals, including some motorized); and hiking. That said, if you prefer fewer neighbors when you camp, here's a little tip that might come in handy: Only 10 miles south is one of the more pleasant (albeit basic) tent-camping sites in the state. I'm referring to the

Hungryman Forest Campground in the northeastern corner of Two Inlets State Forest. The campsites sit along a pine-covered rise above the shores of Hungry Man Lake.

Sites 6–10 at Hungryman are the closest to the water, but all the sites are large, with ample room and vegetation affording privacy. Like most other state forest campgrounds, there are few amenities. Water and vault toilets are the only facilities. Sites are located both inside and outside the loop, with only two sites directly facing each other.

This is a popular fishing and hunting campground, so it will be busy based on those seasonal activities. Because it's only about a 10- or 12-minute ride from the campground to the southern entrance to Lake Itasca, Hungryman Forest Campground offers a refreshing alternative to camping in the state park.

Hungryman Forest Campground

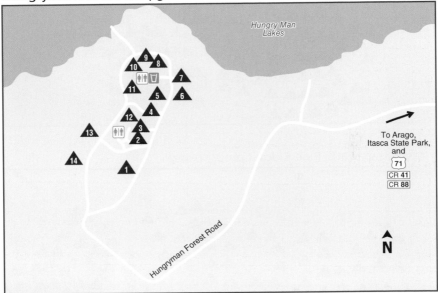

GETTING THERE

To reach Itasca State Park from the intersection of MN 34 and US 71 in Park Rapids, head north on US 71 about 20.5 miles, and turn left onto MN 200. In 0.2 mile turn left (west) onto CR 123/CR 48. Go 1.2 miles, and turn right (north) onto Park Drive/CR 38/CR 1. Enter the park and go 2.4 miles to Campground Road. To reach Pine Ridge Campground, turn right (north) and go 1 mile on Campground Road. To reach Bear Paw Campground, turn left (south) and go 0.5 mile on Campground Road.

To reach the Hungryman Forest Campground from the intersection of MN 34 and US 71 in Park Rapids, head north on US 71 about 11 miles until you get to CR 41 at Arago. Turn left (west), and go 1.1 miles. Turn right (north) onto Becker Line Road, and go 0.6 mile. Turn left (west) and go about 0.5 mile to the campground road on your right. From the intersection of MN 200 and US 71 near Itasca State Park, head south on US 71, and go 9.3 miles. Turn right (west) onto CR 41, and follow the directions above from there. It'll be worth the extra time.

Itasca State Park: Bear Paw Campground

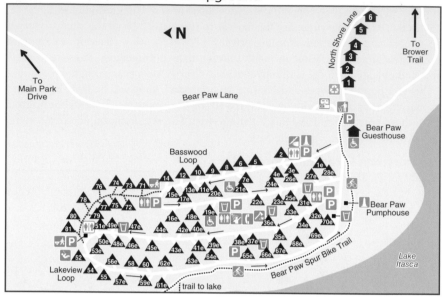

Itasca State Park: Pine Ridge Campground

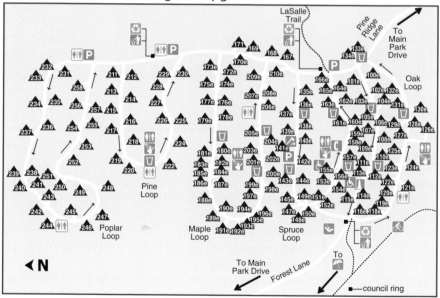

GPS COORDINATES:
  ITASCA STATE PARK CAMPGROUNDS: N47° 13.352' W95° 11.071' (at the intersection for both campground entrances: south to Bear Paw, north to Pine Ridge)
  HUNGRYMAN FOREST CAMPGROUND: N47° 3.546' W95° 11.007'

13

Jay Cooke State Park Campground

Beauty ★★★★ / Privacy ★★★★ / Spaciousness ★★★★ / Quiet ★★★★ / Security ★★★★ / Cleanliness ★★★★

Here are some of the most breathtaking waterfalls and cascades in Minnesota, among a vast network of trails overlooking the river.

Each time I visit Jay Cooke State Park, I am awed by the beauty and unrelenting power of the St. Louis River as it continues to rip and roar through this park. The magnitude of this mighty river and the stark ruggedness of the rocky channel through which it courses are overpowering. The sounds of raging water, the mist rising from each cascading drop and chute—all are testament to the natural forces that continue to form the landscape at this park.

As a hiker, you have your trails cut out for you—more than 50 miles' worth. Crossing the suspension bridge to the southern bank of the river, your choices are as numerous as the different courses of water surging around and over the rocks. Carlton Trail runs along the southern bank for nearly half the length of the park. Others circle down to the river and up through the higher elevations to distant lakes and shelters. You could spend a week hiking all the trails.

The geological history of the park is displayed at every vantage point above the river. Ancient mudflats became the shale that, with the graywacke (a type of sandstone), was exposed during great angular, upward movements of the Earth's crust. Cracks in this upheaved mass were filled in with lava during later geological disturbances. Cooled lava dikes can be seen in the riverbed today. The red clay visible in a widening in the river's gorge is a deposit created by the ancient glacial Lake Duluth that flooded the St. Louis River valley.

Jay Cooke is also noted for its healthy population of Minnesota's larger wildlife residents—deer, black bear, and timber wolf. More than 170 species of birds can be found in the park as well.

Famous footbridge over the raging St. Louis River within the park

courtesy of the Minnesota Department of Natural Resources

KEY INFORMATION

ADDRESS: 780 MN 210, Carlton, MN 55718

CONTACT: 218-673-7000, dnr.state.mn.us/state_parks/jay_cooke

OPERATED BY: Minnesota DNR, Division of Parks and Recreation

OPEN: Year-round (facilities: early May–mid-October)

SITES: 78 (21 with electric), 4 walk-in, 4 backpack-in, 5 camper cabins, 2 walk-in group

EACH SITE HAS: Designated tent-pitching area, picnic table, fire ring

WHEELCHAIR ACCESS: Sites 23, 40, and 57

ASSIGNMENT: Reservations required (same-day reservations available)

REGISTRATION: Reserve at 866-85-PARKS (72757) or tinyurl.com/mnspreservations

FACILITIES: Water, restrooms, showers, water, RV sanitation station

PARKING: 1 vehicle/site (2 vehicles/site with permission); on main campground road on left; at trailhead to group sites

FEES: $23/night, $17/night off-season, $31/night electric sites, $25/night electric sites off-season, $7 daily permit, $35 annual permit, $8.50 reservation fee

---

RESTRICTIONS:

PETS: On 6-foot leash; attended at all times

QUIET HOURS: 10 p.m.–8 a.m.

FIRES: In fire rings; gathering firewood not permitted; firewood must be purchased from approved vendor

ALCOHOL: Not permitted

OTHER: 6 people/site; closed to visitors 10 p.m.–8 a.m.; fireworks and metal detectors prohibited

This part of Minnesota adjacent to the great Lake Superior is also rich in the history of the French fur traders, the voyageurs. Along with Dakota guides, they plied the rivers, traversed the portages, and maintained commercial routes throughout northeastern Minnesota and Canada more than 200 years ago.

The campsites are right across the highway from the park entrance and headquarters, in the heart of the park's amenities. The campground is large, with ample space for each campsite. The entire area is within a dense understory of spruce, cedars, and pines. Campsites are small but tucked into this understory; they provide privacy, quiet, and security to those who camp here. I sensed that these sites might be muddy during heavy rains.

Unlike most state parks, the campsites within the inner circle of all loops are laid out better than most. Interestingly, the first four sites are right inside the entrance, literally before you reach the main campground loop. These, as well as the other half a dozen sites on the right (southern) side of the campground road, are electrical and better suited for the bigger RVs.

Sites 4–23 make up the first loop. These are sites under a scattered canopy of aspens. Sites 7 and 8 have a denser understory than most. Site 11 is a good pick in this loop because it adjoins a rock escarpment and has plenty of space between it and its neighbors on either side. Sites 19 and 20 are long and narrow. This becomes obvious when you look up or down the driveways of either, as they are directly across from each other. Site 23 is wheelchair accessible.

The sites in the second loop (24–37) and third loop (48–63; site 57 is wheelchair accessible) are on the same side of the campground road and are more open, yet the area is thickly wooded with evergreens. Sites 59–64 are very open, offering little privacy. Sites 38–47 (site 40 is wheelchair accessible) are located along a short loop across the road from loop 3. The last drive-in campsites (65–80) are in the fourth or last loop in the series north of the main campground road. Three walk-in sites and three of Jay Cooke's camper cabins are just behind a parking lot on the south side of the campground loops.

My pick for a good site within these loops is 72. It's an outside campsite at the end of the curve on the far loop. It's a long site that extends back into the woods. Just past its driveway is a path leading off to connect with the Civilian Conservation Corps Trail that runs east–west near the northern boundary of the park. This trail connects with several other trails that combine to form a network stretching completely across the park's northern section.

In some areas, the dense screening between sites is due not to a thick understory but to the heavy lower branches of taller spruces and pines that fan out from the trunk and reach down to the ground.

Whitewater rafting is offered just outside the park. Waterfalls and river cascades, an extensive trail system, fishing, and a swinging pedestrian bridge, coupled with the sights and sounds of Jay Cooke State Park, make this an especially sensual north-woods camping experience.

Jay Cooke State Park Campground

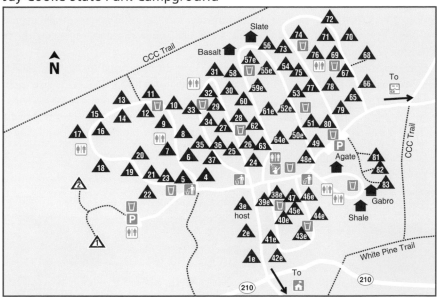

GETTING THERE

From the intersection of MN 210 and MN 45 in Carlton, take MN 210 east 3 miles to the park entrance on the right.

From Duluth take I-35 S to Exit 251B. Head south on MN 23, and in 9 miles turn right onto MN 210. Go west 6.2 miles to the park entrance on the left.

GPS COORDINATES: N46° 39.313' W92° 22.364'

14

McCarthy Beach State Park:
BEATRICE LAKE CAMPGROUND

Beauty ★★ / Privacy ★★★ / Spaciousness ★★★★ / Quiet ★★★ / Security ★★★ / Cleanliness ★★★

Rustic, north-woods campground with rolling hills and views of the lake through the gleaming white trunks of paper birches

Because Beatrice Lake Campground is officially an overflow campground for McCarthy Beach State Park, this may seem like a double listing. But because of its rustic atmosphere and distance from the rest of the activities at the "beach," I feel it deserves a place of its own.

Upon leaving McCarthy Park for Beatrice Lake, one of the first memorable scenes you encounter is a boulevard of towering red pines that grow right to the edge of the road. What's more interesting is that the road's lanes are divided by a center boulevard of pines, so the roadway becomes a narrow corridor overshadowed by giant, stately trees. The effect doesn't last very long, but the image is reminiscent of Lake Itasca and other "avenue of pines" types of roadways. There is a homey, woodsy flavor to the sites, especially the three walk-in sites overlooking the lake.

The campground is laid out along an irregular loop through a mature birch forest dotted with tall red pines and with a solid understory of mixed vegetation. This helps give each site an enclosed, private feeling.

Site 1 sits inside the loop right inside the entrance—a basic site with no real features. Sites 2 and 3 are the first of many in which the lake can be seen in the background. Site 2 has

Beatrice Lake's forested shoreline

KEY INFORMATION

ADDRESS: Beatrice Lake Road, 0.4 mile east of Echo Lane and 0.4 mile west of Cedar Lane, Side Lake, MN 55781

CONTACT: 218-274-7200, dnr.state.mn.us /state_parks/mccarthy_beach

OPERATED BY: Minnesota DNR, Division of Parks and Recreation (managed by McCarthy Beach State Park)

OPEN: Year-round, when accessible

SITES: 27 rustic, 3 walk-in

EACH SITE HAS: Open tent area, picnic table, fire ring

WHEELCHAIR ACCESS: No designated sites

ASSIGNMENT: First come, first serve

REGISTRATION: Self-registration station

FACILITIES: Water, vault toilets

PARKING: 1 vehicle/site; walk-ins park on campground loop near trail to sites; also just past park office and at start of first loop on left

FEES: $15/night, $7 daily permit, $35 annual permit

RESTRICTIONS:

PETS: On 6-foot leash; attended at all times

QUIET HOURS: 10 p.m.–8 a.m.

FIRES: In fire rings; gathering firewood not permitted; firewood must be purchased from approved vendor

ALCOHOL: Not permitted

OTHER: 6 people/site; closed to visitors 10 p.m.–8 a.m.; fireworks and metal detectors prohibited; use of any type of weapon prohibited; no removal of flora or fauna from park

---

trees throughout, whereas site 3 is open and spacious. Site 4 is a standard-issue state park site, and 5 and 6 are very exposed sites right across from each other.

Site 7 sits inside the loop away from the lake, while site 8 sits toward the top of a peninsular knob over the lake and offers campers a filtered view through the trees to the waters beyond. Sites 9 and 10 offer a similar background, although site 9 is very close to the road.

Site 11 sits by itself at the top of the hill and therefore probably has the most open view of the lake from the best perspective thus far. Site 12, across the road, is another average site. The next three sites, 13–15, are laid out very close to each other—more typical of the bigger state parks. Site 16 is the last site at the end of the peninsula and is perched on a ridge overlooking the lake, too. Site 17 is inside the loop and can be seen fairly easily from neighboring sites.

Sites 18–20 are the most remote as they all sit back off the road on a knob of land that juts out to define a small bay at the northern end of the lake. These sites are close enough together that they are not going to feel truly remote, but the fact that they are off the main road means if you have several campers with tents in your party you might be able to secure these three sites as your own group site. Sites 18–20 are the designated walk-in sites. There is a small parking turnout on the right, at the trailhead into the walk-in area.

Site 21 captures a bit of this little bay's charm and is one of the most picturesque campsites in this loop. Site 22 overlooks the lake and site 21 but isn't so close as to be overly intrusive. Of the last eight sites, only site 24 has a notable view of the lake. The others are stretched around a loop.

This was a simple state forest campground before being turned into an overflow site by the park to the south. I wouldn't let that keep you from checking out this area first, as it's more rustic than McCarthy and yet close enough to reap all the benefits of that developed park, including its swimming beach.

Boaters will find that the easiest access to the lake is via a public boat ramp just west of the campground entrance on Beatrice Lake Road. Both canoeists and kayakers will find that the lake's undulating shoreline offers myriad opportunities for exploration.

About 0.5 mile outside the entrance to the east, Beatrice Lake Road intersects with a section of the Taconite State Trail. This trail connects with others within McCarthy Beach State Park to the south.

If you don't need additional amenities, you'll find Beatrice Lake overflowing with inviting campsites.

McCarthy Beach State Park: Beatrice Lake Campground

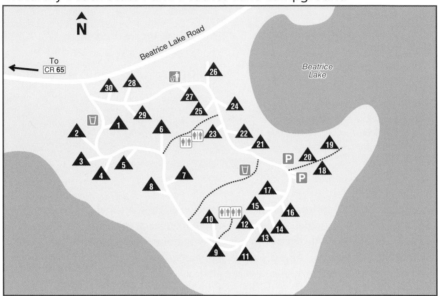

GETTING THERE

From the intersection of US 169 and MN 37 in Hibbing take US 169 north 6.6 miles. Turn right onto MN 73, and in 0.7 mile turn left onto CR 5. Go 15 miles, and turn left (west) onto McCarthy Beach Road, which becomes Link Lake Trail. In 5.9 miles turn right onto Beatrice Lake Road. Go about 1 mile to the entrance to Beatrice Lake on the right. An alternative route is to stay on CR 5 another 3.2 miles, and turn left onto Snake Trail Road. In 2.5 miles turn left onto Beatrice Lake Road, and go about 1 mile to the campground entrance on the left.

GPS COORDINATES: N47° 42.655′ W93° 4.307′

15

McCarthy Beach State Park:
SIDE LAKE CAMPGROUND

Beauty ★★ / Privacy ★★★ / Spaciousness ★★★ / Quiet ★★ / Security ★★★ / Cleanliness ★★★

This long, clear-water, north-woods beach has extensive trails through a pine forest and features rather unusual campsite landscaping.

The unique layout of the campground and a few high-ranking sites are two good reasons to camp at McCarthy Beach. This is a park for those who like to play in or on the water. The long sandy beach is a landmark in these parts, and the amenities clearly support all kinds of water-based activities. The campground is actually laid out on Side Lake, across the road from the beach area. Both lakes have boat ramps, are excellent for fishing (Side Lake has two fishing piers for campers to use), and provide plenty of shoreline for exploration in canoes and kayaks.

There are 18 miles of hiking trails within the park, all stretched out along the interior of the northern half. These trails form long, interconnecting loops that traverse the glacial topography as they wind among towering stands of pine trees. Hikers can also hook up with the Taconite State Trail, which threads its way through this park and adjoining state forests.

The picnic area and sandy shoreline at McCarthy Beach

courtesy of the Minnesota Department of Natural Resources

KEY INFORMATION

ADDRESS: 7622 McCarthy Beach Road, Side Lake, MN 55781

CONTACT: 218-274-7200, dnr.state.mn.us /state_parks/mccarthy_beach

OPERATED BY: Minnesota DNR, Division of Parks and Recreation

OPEN: April–late November (facilities: mid-May–mid-October, depending on weather)

SITES: 58 (21 with electric) (Note: Beatrice Lake is managed as a second campground unit.)

EACH SITE HAS: Open tent area, picnic table, fire ring

WHEELCHAIR ACCESS: Sites 2, 12, 19, 21

ASSIGNMENT: Reservations required (same-day reservations available)

REGISTRATION: Reserve at 866-85-PARKS (72757) or tinyurl.com/mnspreservations

FACILITIES: Showers, fishing pier, boat ramp, water, vault toilets

PARKING: 1 vehicle/site; just past park office and at start of first loop

FEES: Side Lake Campground: $23/night, $17/night off-season, $31/night electric sites, $7 daily permit, $35 annual permit, $8.50 reservation fee

RESTRICTIONS:

PETS: On 6-foot leash; attended at all times

QUIET HOURS: 10 p.m.–8 a.m.

FIRES: In fire rings; gathering firewood not permitted; firewood must be purchased from approved vendor

ALCOHOL: Not permitted

OTHER: 6 people/site; closed to visitors 10 p.m.–8 a.m.; fireworks and metal detectors prohibited

Birders can see more than 170 species of birds throughout the park at different times of the year, and Sturgeon Lake, nearly 2 miles across at its widest, offers anglers a chance to catch walleye, bass, northern pike, and panfish.

Now, on to the campgrounds. The first loop, sites 1–13 (sites 2 and 12 are wheelchair accessible), consists of electrical hookup sites; leave those for the RVs. The second loop gets a little better, but the configuration makes for tight sites with little privacy. Three roads intersect the loop, cutting it into quarters. These sites are all open with little understory, and they back up to other sites within this loop network. Sites 19 and 21 are wheelchair accessible. Site 42 is a large, open site with a clear view of the lake—go for it in a pinch, and only if the last loop is full.

Ah, the last loop—very interesting! There's some major landscaping incorporated into some of the sites in this section. Many of them have extensive stone retaining walls that either define the tent and table area or secure the driveway or approaches to the sites. All the sites are spacious, so the landscaping further individualizes the campsite, making each one unique.

Site 47, on the roadway between the second and third loops, sits in front of an embankment fortified by a long, 4-foot-tall wall of stones. The site sits above the roadway, offering a good view of the lake across the road. It's exposed, so it's not very private. Sites 48 and 49 are inside the loop and about 50 yards from the lake. Because this loop angles back away from the lake slightly, these two sites are the closest to the water.

Site 50 is cut back into a grove of birch and aspen, a truly private yet spacious site outside the loop. Sites 51 and 52 are fairly close but roomy, with good understory screening. This area underwent extensive site work and tree removal as part of a storm cleanup a few years ago. Site 55 sits on a knoll, with an elaborate stone retaining wall keeping it all together. The next three sites, 56–58, vary in size (site 56 is small but nice; 57 has a sloping camping area; and 58 is long and narrow). Site 59 features landscape timbers and a boulder-lined stairway—with a view of the lake filtered through a stand of pines.

This area was once covered in dense white and red pine forests. There are many small stands of these pines scattered throughout the campground and park. The carpet of needles on the forest floor was one of the thickest and softest coverings I have ever walked over. The pines in this area and those lining the county road that runs through the park reminded me of Lake Itasca at times.

At the extreme northwestern edge of the park lies Beatrice Lake Campground, a state forest–area campground that could serve as a remote and even more rustic overflow option for the McCarthy Beach campground (it earns a listing of its own on page 52). Even if you don't intend to camp there, consider a drive up to Beatrice Lake. There is a small section of the road that is a red pine boulevard—the lanes are narrow and separated by a raised center section. Towering red pines grow right up to the roadway's edge, and the center corridor is thick with more majestic trees. It's quite a sight.

Make sure you bring your beach toys, fishing gear, and hiking boots on this camping trip!

McCarthy Beach State Park: Side Lake Campground

GETTING THERE

From the intersection of US 169 and MN 37 in Hibbing take US 169 north 6.6 miles. Turn right onto MN 73, and in 0.7 mile turn left onto CR 5. Go 15 miles, and turn left (west) onto McCarthy Beach Road. Go 1.1 miles , and the park entrance will be on the left.

GPS COORDINATES: N47° 40.248' W93° 1.864'

16

⚠ Mosomo Point Campground

Beauty ★★★ / Privacy ★★★★★ / Spaciousness ★★★★★ / Quiet ★★★ / Security ★★★★ / Cleanliness ★★★★

This unimposing, serene, primitive campground sits in the heart of a beautiful, lake-filled forest.

This tent-campground area is included for one simple reason: Mosomo Point caught my eye with its sheer simplicity and its incredibly large, long, and deep campsites. I felt as if I had pitched my tent in the sloping waterfront yard of a friend's cabin. There was enough room at the site I selected to pitch at least a half dozen tents and still have room for a round of lawn bowling. It was a pleasant surprise to me, because I had spent an entire summer in this area working as a student forester for the Minnesota Department of Natural Resources but had never visited the Lake Winnie area, where Mosomo Point (one of several national forest campgrounds in the region) is located.

"A wide-open, grassy clearing, surrounded by towering red pines" describes these camp-sites. Each site has ample grass-covered, flat areas for numerous tents and myriad lawn games. The long, narrow, lakeside campsites are separated from the lake by a thick, reed-bound shoreline. The reed bed extends out into the lake for several yards. However, each site has direct access to the open water for fishing or launching a boat. Boaters have access to the waters of Big Cut Foot Sioux Lake, which surrounds the point on three sides. From there the routes connecting to other lakes are almost endless. This is a popular access point for fishermen, so expect traffic to be heavy and sites at a premium during the opening week-end of fishing season and times of heavy fishing success.

The waters of Lake Winnibigoshish at Mosomo Point

KEY INFORMATION

ADDRESS: 45033 MN 46, Deer River, MN 56636

CONTACT: 218-246-2123, tinyurl.com /mosomopointcg

OPERATED BY: Chippewa National Forest, Deer River District

OPEN: Early May–mid-September

SITES: 22

EACH SITE HAS: Open tent area, picnic table, fire ring

WHEELCHAIR ACCESS: No designated sites

ASSIGNMENT: All reservable

REGISTRATION: Box at entrance; reserve at 877-444-6777 or recreation.gov

FACILITIES: Vault toilets, water, recycling station, boat access

PARKING: 1 vehicle/site

FEES: $16/night

RESTRICTIONS:

PETS: On leash only

QUIET HOURS: 10 p.m.–6 a.m.

FIRES: In fire rings; gathering downed or dead firewood permitted; firewood must be purchased from approved vendor

ALCOHOL: Permitted

OTHER: 8 people/site; use the facilities provided, such as tent pads and latrines; water faucets for collecting water only—do not use area to wash dishes, fish, or other items; noise limits enforced at developed sites

The sites at Mosomo are the largest I've seen anywhere, bar none: state parks, state forests, and private campgrounds. There is no distinction between tent-only and RV sites, but because there are no RV facilities, the only advantage that Mosomo can offer is the incredibly long corridor beyond the driveway at each site. The standard-issue picnic table and grill-topped fire ring are the extent of the "improvements" you'll find here. Each site's dense understory blocks the view from distant campsites and the road through the camp itself. These sites are, indeed, off the chart for spaciousness and privacy.

Of course the area is beautiful and picturesque—after all, it is the Chippewa National Forest. With more than 660,000 acres of forest, including the dominant white, red, and jack pine forests; dense stands of northern hardwoods; 1,300-plus lakes; 920-plus miles of streams; and 440,000 acres of wetlands, this forest is home to some of the best scenery, flora, and fauna that Minnesota has to offer. Mosomo Point provides easy access to a number of waterways and connecting lakes on the east side of Lake Winnie.

As is the case with most of the campgrounds in the Chippewa and Superior National Forests, water plays a dominant role and is clearly the focal point of most of the recreational options. Whether for fishing or paddling, these modest campgrounds are the jumping-off places for enjoying hundreds of miles of streams, lakes, and faraway reaches of water. If the waters surrounding the Mosomo Point peninsula don't satisfy your aquatic needs, there's always Lake Winnibigoshish and its other watery neighbors. The not-yet-mighty-at-this-point Mississippi River is still a relatively small stream where it spills out of Lake Winnie near here on its meandering flow southward. Mosomo Point is among several campgrounds in the immediate vicinity that are cut out of the forest—right at the water's edge. Many are connected by the same network of waterways too.

Birders should be aware of the resident population of bald eagles that call the Chippewa home. More than 150 breeding pairs have been counted in these trees. It's not uncommon to hear the imposing whoof-whoof-whoof of gigantic wing beats overhead as these mighty birds power out from the shadows and swoop out over the meadows.

The Cut Foot Sioux area also has numerous nonmotorized trails and plenty of local wildlife (ospreys, loons, deer) to keep animal- and bird-watchers busy. Activities include fishing and boating.

Very heavy usage and potential traffic noise are the two biggest drawbacks to this campground. Motorboat traffic from nearby lodges and the fluctuating level of traffic noise from the state highway have the potential for creating a subtle and almost unnoticeable commercial drone in the background. That annoyance lasts only until that first loon begins to call. It seemed to me that its call echoed within my tall-pines hideaway all night long.

Mosomo Point Campground

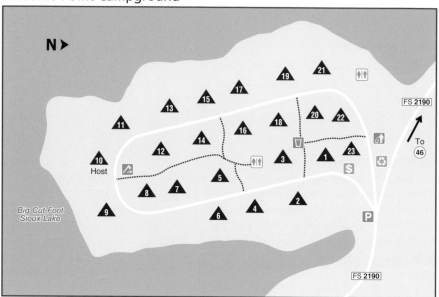

GETTING THERE

From Bena take US 2 east 1.5 miles to CR 9. Turn left (north) and go 11 miles to MN 46. Turn left (north) on MN 46, and drive 6.6 miles to the campground sign (FS 2190). Turn left into the campground.

GPS COORDINATES: N47° 31.557' W94° 2.508'

17

North Star Campground

Beauty ★★★ / Privacy ★★★ / Spaciousness ★★★★ / Quiet ★★★ / Security ★★★★ / Cleanliness ★★★★

This spacious campground is right on one of the most scenic drives in Minnesota.

I hadn't been seeking this campground when I sped by it heading back south after a long weekend of checking out the northeastern section of the Chippewa National Forest. Instead, I was enjoying the 200-year-old pine forests and other natural sites along the Northwoods Scenic Byway, a beautiful corridor along MN 38 that extends 40 miles between Grand Rapids and Bigfork. Don't expect a lot of commercial amenities along this route—take the opportunity to explore side roads throughout the Chippewa National Forest and the George Washington State Forest.

I saw the NATIONAL FOREST CAMPGROUND sign and immediately fanned through my pile of reference papers and maps on the seat beside me. North Star Campground hadn't jumped off the page the first time around because its list of amenities pretty much stopped at "lake." What a lucky break for us all. North Star Campground is definitely a good find.

The sites are laid out along a bisected kidney-shaped loop nestled into an aspen and balsam fir forest sandwiched between the state road and the shores of the lake.

Stairway landing at campsite above North Star Lake

KEY INFORMATION

ADDRESS: 46891 MN 38, Marcell, MN 56657

CONTACT: 218-246-2123, tinyurl.com /northstarcg

OPERATED BY: Chippewa National Forest, Deer River Ranger District

OPEN: Year-round, when accessible (facilities: early May–late September)

SITES: 36 rustic

EACH SITE HAS: Open tent area, picnic table, fire ring

WHEELCHAIR ACCESS: No designated sites

ASSIGNMENT: First come, first served; no reservations

REGISTRATION: Box at entrance

FACILITIES: Vault toilet, drinking water, playground, boat ramp, swimming beach

PARKING: 1 vehicle/site; also by swimming area

FEES: $14/night

RESTRICTIONS:

PETS: On leash only

QUIET HOURS: 10 p.m.–6 a.m.

FIRES: In fire rings; gathering downed or dead firewood permitted; firewood must be purchased from approved vendor

ALCOHOL: Permitted

OTHER: 8 people/site; use the facilities provided, such as tent pads and latrines; noise limits enforced at developed sites

Sites 1 and 2 are long, narrow keyhole sites that open up to a stand of aspens and balsam fir at the end of long driveways. Site 3 is off the inside of the loop but centrally located to facilities and the lake itself. There is no site 4—look for the firewood bin where you'd expect another tent site.

Site 5 is another long, narrow site and neighbors the campground host at site 6. Sites 8 and 9 overlook North Star Lake. Both sites are open to the road, but the view compensates for the lack of privacy. There is also a trail down to the lake just before the driveway to 7.

Just before site 9 there is a turnoff to the parking area at the trailhead that leads to the swimming area at the beach. The campsite right after the parking lot is on a slight rise surrounded by more understory than grass, unlike most other sites at North Star Lake.

Site 10, although it is located inside the loop, is far enough off the road to reward campers with more privacy than most other sites in this loop. Sites 12–14 are fairly open but are especially friendly and spacious nonetheless. The angled and staggered driveways give each site ample screening from others and from the roadway. Sites 15 and 16 are keyhole-designed driveways and sites—a plus because the entrances to these two sites sit opposite each other. The rest of the sites in this left (southern) half of the loop all retain the sense of privacy and spaciousness that is most characteristic of the campground. Site 19 is especially appealing, if only for the fact that it's back in the woods and is the last site on the outside edge. Although I didn't detect any noise, I would suspect that these last few sites might put campers within heightened earshot of road noise from MN 38, just outside the campgrounds.

The other half of the loop, the northern section, is cut through a younger stand of aspen, spruce, and fir trees. Most of these sites are in the keyhole style, similar to those in the other half of the loop. The inside loop offers a pleasant change: its sites are cut out of a dense understory and are quite private and very well protected from each other and the road. Much of the screening between campsites and the background understory is provided by a young spruce forest that blankets this area.

Sites 22–31 are similar in layout and appearance. Site 28 is centrally located within the loop, connected by foot trails and within easy reach of the toilets and water pump.

Site 32 is the first spot in this half of the loop that could be described as being on the lake. It's a beautiful campsite overlooking North Star Lake, and the site has its own stairway and trail leading down to the lake's shoreline. In fact, all the sites along the ridge above the lake have stairways or trails leading right down to the water. Of these sites, 33 is the most exposed. A trail cuts to the lake between sites 35 and 36.

The road turns away from the lake at site 36. The remaining sites are uniformly narrow compared to the majority of the keyhole sites in the campground.

North Star Lake is more than 1,000 acres in area and is at least 3 miles long. It appears on the map as an irregularly edged, inverted Y and is known for its myriad sheltered bays and ever-wavering shoreline. There are numerous sandy and grassy beaches throughout. Anglers can try their luck catching walleye, northern pike, and muskie as well as bluegills, crappie, and bass. Campers can also enjoy swimming and canoeing. North Star Lake is like a small, simply faceted gem sitting unnoticed in a big jewelry box.

North Star Campground

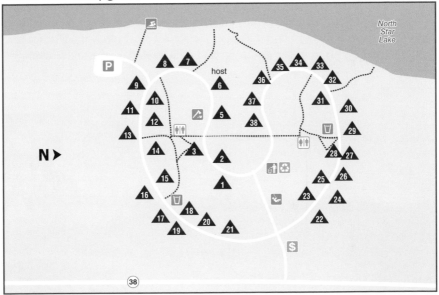

GETTING THERE

From Marcell head south 3 miles on MN 38 to the campground on the right (west) side of the road.

GPS COORDINATES: N47° 33.433' W93° 39.078'

Owen Lake Campground

Beauty ★★★★ / Privacy ★★★★★ / Spaciousness ★★★★★ / Quiet ★★★ / Security ★★★ / Cleanliness ★★★★

This modest campground on a red pine–forested peninsula features a pleasantly perfect lakeside campsite.

Owen Lake is one of those rare finds that makes doing a camping guide so rewarding. Initially I had traveled to this somewhat bleak area of Minnesota, a region of vast spruce swamps and endless miles of nondescript forest roads to check out Scenic State Park. I was underwhelmed by that campground, so I decided to see if the state forest sites were as pleasant in this remote area as they were elsewhere. I am so glad I did.

Owen Lake is a beautiful, irregularly shaped northern lake with several bays and bumps along its shoreline. Nestled under a healthy stand of red pines on a peninsula jutting out from the lake's western shore is the state forest campground.

Getting to Owen Lake means several miles of paved, then gravel, roads through impressive stands of red pine. The campground is likewise under an umbrella of red pine with an understory of both young red and jack pine. All the sites are laid out along a long, narrow loop that extends toward the peninsula's point. Sites are spread apart nicely to allow for privacy, and even those sites away from the lake are an easy walk across the loop to the beach.

Owen Lake from the campground

KEY INFORMATION

ADDRESS: 55379 Owen Lake Campground Road, Bigfork, MN 56628

CONTACT: 218-743-3362, dnr.state.mn.us /state_forests/facilities/cmp00024

OPERATED BY: George Washington State Forest (managed by Scenic State Park)

OPEN: Year-round (mid-May–late October; no fees or garbage pickup in winter, but vault toilets and well are year-round)

SITES: 17 rustic, 2 walk-in

EACH SITE HAS: Open tent area, picnic table, fire ring

WHEELCHAIR ACCESS: Site 8

ASSIGNMENT: First come, first served; no reservations

REGISTRATION: Required; envelopes provided

FACILITIES: Vault toilet, water, picnic pavilion

PARKING: 1 vehicle/site; across from picnic area; at trailhead to sites 9 and 10; just before site 11

FEES: $14/night

RESTRICTIONS:

PETS: On 6-foot leash; attended at all times

QUIET HOURS: 10 p.m.–8 a.m.

FIRES: In fire rings; gathering downed and dead firewood permitted; firewood must be purchased from approved vendor

ALCOHOL: Not permitted

OTHER: 8 people/site; closed to visitors 10 p.m.–8 a.m.

Site 1 is in a grove of red pine but not situated close enough to the lake to claim that as a feature. Sites 2 and 3 back up to the lake and could be a combination or group site because there is little screening between the two. Sites 4 and 5 are long, narrow sites that go back into the pines for spacious and private camping. Site 6 is on the lake but exposed to the road.

The nicest site on the lake is 7, but don't expect to camp there—it's used all summer by the campground host. You'll have to settle for site 8 (wheelchair accessible), off by itself amid the jack pine understory.

Just past site 8, the loop swings left, with a parking turnout on the right. This is the trailhead for the two walk-in sites, 9 and 10. These sites require that you carry all your gear into camp. It will be worth it—even if it means lugging the 50-pound cooler 50 yards. This peninsula has an open understory with a mature red pine forest and a panoramic view of the lake.

Site 9 is just off the road and therefore more immediately accessible. It is far enough from site 10 to offer more privacy than most, but expect some trail use as campers at site 10 and other visitors explore this point.

Site 10—what can I say? It's under a tall stand of straight, lean red pines with an open, pine needle–covered forest floor. There are a few jack pines scattered throughout, and scattered paper birches add north country charm. The end of the peninsula rises to form a modest knoll above the water. The campground is completely exposed to those approaching from the main loop, but it's so spacious that one can turn toward the lake and forget about everything else. Water and toilets are back on the loop, only a campsite down from the trailhead.

The lake to the east is very inviting for canoeing or kayaking. It appears to offer several miles of undeveloped shoreline, typical of many northern lakes. Immediately across from the campground there are a few cabins lining the shore.

Site 11 begins the series of campsites on the loop away from the water. There is a private residence behind site 11. This spot, however, does sit in the red pines and is screened from the private property beyond.

Sites 13 and 14 are basic campsites and feature those common amenities of picnic table, fire ring, and tent space. Sites 15–18 are big, open sites and therefore roomy but very private compared to others. Sites 19 and 20 are close to the road and nondescript.

It is truly unfortunate that there are not more sites like number 10. Plan your trip to arrive early and secure it for a real camping treat.

There are scores of fishing and boating lakes, many with campgrounds, surrounding Owen Lake. The George Washington State Forest, in which Owen Lake is located, is just northeast of the Chippewa National Forest's extensive lake region. All these areas offer camping, but none offer the beauty and grandness of site 10 at Owen Lake. Activities include fishing, swimming, canoeing, and kayaking. Treat yourself: check it out.

Owen Lake Campground

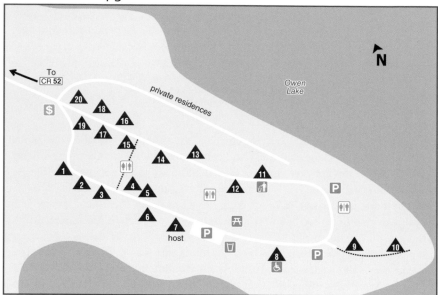

GETTING THERE

From Bigfork take Scenic Highway/CR 7 southeast 9.6 miles to CR 340. Turn left (east) and go 6.5 miles to CR 52. Then turn left (north) and follow the signs about 1.5 miles to Lost Lake Trail. Turn left (west) and go 1.6 miles to the campground road on the right. The campground is 0.4 mile east.

GPS COORDINATES: N47° 40.705' W93° 23.649'

19

Savanna Portage State Park Campground

Beauty ★★★ / Privacy ★★★ / Spaciousness ★★★ / Quiet ★★★ / Security ★★★ / Cleanliness ★★★

Relive the lifestyle of voyageurs of yore while you enjoy north-woods camping in lake country.

You can look at Savanna Portage from a couple of perspectives: you can observe the north-woods lake country sculpted by glaciers that formed lakes, bogs, and rolling hillside, or you can envision brightly clad French fur traders and other voyageurs portaging heavy canoes and gear half a dozen miles through shallow streams and across expansive mudflats—and then through several miles of virgin northern forest. Such is the dual personality of this park.

Glacially speaking, Savanna Portage is an example of how some river country was formed. When huge ice fields retreated, they left great moraine fields at their leading edge. These ridges of rock blocked flowages from melting ice until at some weak point they broke through, creating channels through which rivers could run. These connecting river systems, first learned and traveled by American Indians, became the water routes and portages that ultimately linked the Great Lakes and points east to the Mississippi River and the great interior of North America.

There are many places within this park to experience what these early canoeists went through to move their boats and gear across the continent. There are several lakes within

Boat launch and fishing pier on Shumway Lake

KEY INFORMATION

ADDRESS: 55626 Lake Place, McGregor, MN 55760 (campground is 1.5 miles east on Shumway Lake Road)

CONTACT: 218-426-3271, dnr.state.mn.us /state_parks/savanna_portage

OPERATED BY: Minnesota DNR, Division of Parks and Recreation

OPEN: Year-round (facilities: mid-May–mid-October)

SITES: 60 (18 with electric), 7 backpack-in, 2 canoe-in, 1 camper cabin, 1 guesthouse, 1 group

EACH SITE HAS: Open tent area, picnic table, fire ring

WHEELCHAIR ACCESS: Sites 33, 42, and 61

ASSIGNMENT: Reservations required, except 2 backpack-in and 1 canoe-in, which are first come, first served (same-day reservations available)

REGISTRATION: Reserve at 866-85-PARKS (72757) or tinyurl.com/mnspreservations

FACILITIES: Boat ramp, dock, fishing pier, play field, restrooms (flush and vault toilets), showers, water, RV sanitation station

PARKING: 1 vehicle/site

FEES: $21/night, $17/night off-season, $29/ night electric sites, $7 daily permit, $35 annual permit, $8.50 reservation fee

RESTRICTIONS:

PETS: On 6-foot leash; attended at all times

QUIET HOURS: 10 p.m.–8 a.m.

FIRES: In fire rings; gathering firewood not permitted; firewood must be purchased from approved vendor

ALCOHOL: Not permitted

OTHER: 6 people/site; closed to visitors 10 p.m.–8 a.m.; fireworks and metal detectors prohibited; electric motors only on Loon, Wolf, and Shumway Lakes

the park's boundaries, as well as remote camping sites that are accessible only by walking along a trail or paddling to the site.

The 61 campsites are laid out between two elongated loops on the southwestern edge of Shumway Lake. A winding road through a random spattering of glacial hills covered in older aspens and surrounded by tamarack swamps greets visitors as they approach these sites.

The campground is situated on a high ridge under an umbrella of aspens mixed with balsam firs. The sites are typical state-park issue: picnic table, fire ring, and place for tent. Some sites are open in a stand of pines (site 3); some have long, narrow driveways (site 7). About half of the sites in the first loop are electrical, so expect them to be in high demand by the mechanized campers. Once you get halfway around the loop, you begin to see the lake through the trees. Sites 26 and 27 are situated on the outside edge of the loop, with the lake behind them. A trail extends from the road just before site 27 and leads to an intersection with a trail that continues around Shumway Lake and also connects to other trail systems in the park. These two sites are especially choice spots and will go quickly. The rest of the sites to the end of the first loop are also electrical sites.

The second loop is laid out parallel to the lake, not right at its edge but viewable through the trees. The first sites in this loop are exposed, right off the roadway, providing no privacy. Lakeside sites 41–45 are small but quaint, each overlooking the lake beyond the screen of trees. The exception is site 42; it's across the road and has a pull-through driveway because it is one of three wheelchair-accessible sites in this park.

There is a rental cabin right off the loop by sites 51 and 53. The rest of the sites along the upper edge of the loop are typical, with the exception of site 58, which is off by itself and private. Likewise, site 60 is situated up from the road and right across from site 61, which is also accessible to disabled campers.

The group site is a spacious, grassy opening across from the road running through the first loop. Sites 62–64 are exposed to each other beneath a canopy of mature red and white pines. Site 63 backs up to site 60 in the second loop, and 64 is off to the west with woods as its backdrop.

Even though this park's theme is based on the voyageur heritage, it could easily be called a hiker's park as well. There are more than 22 miles of hiking trails, many of which encircle the lakes within the park. You can even hike part of the original Savanna Portage—modernized with a wood-plank walkway through one of the swampy areas. The Continental Divide Trail brings hikers along part of the divide that sends water on one side ultimately to the Atlantic, and on the other, south to the Gulf of Mexico.

The park lies within the boundary of Savanna State Forest, so trails extend beyond the park, creating a network that offers many multilooped routes, some leading to remote lakes.

The lakes have resident northern pike, trout, bass, and panfish. I first camped at Savanna Portage more than 20 years ago and spent a whole day just whiling away the time in my canoe. There are plenty of activities: swimming, fishing, canoeing, kayaking, hiking, mountain biking, and more. Canoes, kayaks, and boats are available for rent in season, and snowshoes can be rented in winter. Such water activities and a good set of hiking boots will keep campers at Savanna Portage primed with options throughout their stay.

Savanna Portage State Park Campground

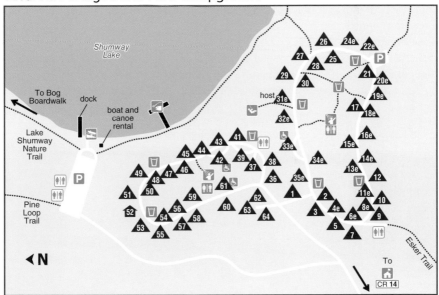

GETTING THERE

From McGregor take MN 65 north 7 miles to Lake Avenue/CR 14. Turn right and continue northeast 10.3 miles to the park entrance. It's another 1.5 miles to the campground.

GPS COORDINATES: N46° 49.587' W93° 9.085'

20

Sawbill Lake Campground

Beauty ★★★ / Privacy ★★★ / Spaciousness ★★★ / Quiet ★★★ / Security ★★★ / Cleanliness ★★★

This hub of activity is a major entry point for canoe trips into the Boundary Waters Canoe Area Wilderness and has north-woods charm—a beautiful lake, towering pines, and memorable scenery.

The Sawbill Trail—it has that boundary waters ring to it, like the Gunflint and the Echo, names that conjure up canoeing across long, pine-forested lakes in God's country. There are many campsites stretched out along the perimeter of the Boundary Waters Canoe Area Wilderness (BWCAW) but few nicer and more convenient than the Sawbill Lake Campground, sitting almost halfway along the BWCAW's southern boundary.

While most campers are probably overnighting at Sawbill before heading out on that canoe trip of a lifetime, there are probably as many others who have come to enjoy the waterways of Sawbill Lake and beyond for a weekend of paddling. The campground features plenty of amenities to satisfy even the noncanoeist in a group: bass and northern pike fishing off the barrier-free fishing pier; a short nature trail along the lake and looped through the campgrounds; and even a genuine north-woods canoe outfitter right next door—a real hub of activity offering canoes, paddles, showers, groceries, and throngs of canoeists from all across the country.

The campground is a long loop divided into quarters along a ridge above the lake. The first campsite sits right off the entrance and seems more like a sentry post than a campsite—in location, not features. It's right across from the canoe storage area, a convenient, shoreside area where you can keep your canoe instead of lugging it up to camp every day.

Canoeists heading out from the boat launch near the campground

photographed by Brian Henry

KEY INFORMATION

ADDRESS: 4620 Sawbill Trail, Tofte, MN 55615

CONTACT: 218-663-7150, sawbill.com/www /campgrounds/sawbill; tinyurl.com/sawbill lakecg

OPERATED BY: Superior National Forest, Tofte Ranger District (managed by Sawbill Canoe Outfitters)

OPEN: May–October (no services or fees in winter)

SITES: 50

EACH SITE HAS: Open tent area, picnic table, fire ring

WHEELCHAIR ACCESS: 3 barrier-free accessible sites (1 in main campground, 2 in separate campground spur)

ASSIGNMENT: 25 first come, first served; 25 reservable

REGISTRATION: At Sawbill Canoe Outfitters

FACILITIES: Vault toilet, water, trash container, canoe storage area

PARKING: 1 vehicle/site; second vehicle $9 additional fee; maximum 2 vehicles/site; all vehicles must be on parking spurs; also at fishing pier and to right of campground entrance at Sawbill Canoe Outfitters

FEES: $18/night

RESTRICTIONS:

PETS: Under owner's control at all times

QUIET HOURS: 10 p.m.–6 a.m.; no loud music

FIRES: In fire rings; gathering downed or dead firewood permitted; firewood must be purchased from approved vendor; non-ash firewood gathered within 100 miles of Superior National Forest permitted

ALCOHOL: Permitted

OTHER: 9 people/site; use the facilities provided, such as tent pads and latrines; dispose of garbage in containers provided; noise limits enforced at developed sites; nonmotorized boats only on Sawbill Lake

---

The terrain is hilly and covered in a mix of spruces and pines. The campground road climbs up a ridge as it leaves site 1 and presents sites 2 and 3 off a Y driveway on the right. These sites are in a stand of birch and balsam but are otherwise open, offering little privacy. Site 4 is likewise open and sits across from site 5, which does overlook the lake. This is a site worth noting for the big red pine trees throughout.

Sites 6–9 are all decent in size and location, each being a short distance from the road and each under a canopy of giant red pines. These are older forests without much understory. Tent sites 14 and 16–18 border the lake and are set back from the road but still quite open, meaning minimal privacy. However, the view down to the lake through the rustic red columns of pines gives these sites their real value. Site 13 is typical of the sites throughout the park, although it is on the small side.

Sites 19–21 are close to the road, but the stands of red pine are impressive. The fact that there is minimal understory or other screening between the sites is unimportant because the canopy above is so impressive that no one's bothering to look into other camps—they are gazing into the treetops.

A trail crossing the road just before 21 is part of the campground loop that follows the lake from the canoe storage area to the shoreline below site 21. It cuts through to the outside loop at site 34 and follows the campground road back down past site 45 before it cuts back through the campground to the lake just below campsites 10 and 12.

Sites 22 and 23 are on opposite sides of the road—open, but secluded. Site 24 is a small site but is off by itself inside the curve as the road cuts away from the lake and the remaining 26 sites.

At the tip of the curve sits site 26, with its long, narrow driveway leading to a very isolated campsite. Better to stay at this one than its neighbor: site 27 is way too exposed and sits at the Y intersection with the outer campground road and the spur to CR 2 that heads north from the campsites.

Campsites 30–39 are staggered along the loop, with most of the sites on the outside of the circle. These sites, with a few exceptions, are long and narrow with a pleasing understory dominated by balsam fir. Sites to avoid are 35 (very small) and 36 (open and in a clearing).

By site 44, the forest is mainly white pine. The site to shy away from here is 49 because it backs up, nearly tent-stake-to-tent-stake, with site 6 on the first loop. The sites have an open understory and a direct line from driveway to driveway right through the middle of the camping area. The last site in this campground is 50, a big site alone among the pines.

Activities include fishing, swimming, hiking, and fantastic paddling in the BWCAW. As either a canoe country starting point or as a base camp for local exploring, Sawbill Lake is a great north-woods canoe country campground.

Sawbill Lake Campground

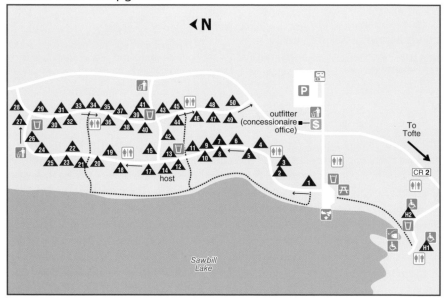

GETTING THERE

From the intersection of MN 61 and Sawbill Trail/CR 2 in Tofte, head north on Sawbill Trail/CR 2. Go 22.5 miles to the campground entrance. Turn left toward the boat launch area and then right into the campground.

GPS COORDINATES: N47° 51.801' W90° 53.240'

21

Spirit Mountain Campground

Beauty ★★★ / Privacy ★★★ / Spaciousness ★★★ / Quiet ★★★ / Security ★★★ / Cleanliness ★★★★

Campsites are nestled into the tree-covered ridgetops high above the St. Louis River bay at the western tip of Lake Superior.

Spirit Mountain is the only private, nonagency campground in this guide. I had omitted it from the initial edition because I assumed that it would follow the pattern of most commercially driven campgrounds in the state: space is money. To my delight, I found that the true spirit of camping is alive and well at Spirit Mountain campgrounds.

However, I must qualify that by adding that 39 of the 68 campsites favor RV use. There aren't enough level areas—or even adequate space—at some sites to pitch a tent without taking up breathing room around the campfire and picnic table.

However, the network of sites laid out along the ridgetop under a canopy of oak and maple forest creates a pleasant, rustic atmosphere for tents and RVs alike. For this critique of sites, I picked out only those that I felt are amply suitable for tent camping. These include sites with level tent-pitching areas, good cover, and understory screening. Because of the landscape high above the St. Louis valley cutting into the western shores of Lake Superior, this campground has a special high-country presence about it.

All of these sites are laid out within a densely forested stand of stately hardwood trees. This is a lush, woodsy campground, so most sites have the luxury of shade and screening.

A roomy, wooded campsite in the maple forests of Spirit Mountain

KEY INFORMATION

ADDRESS: 9535 W. Skyline Parkway, Duluth, MN 55810

CONTACT: 218-624-8544; 800-642-6377, ext. 544; spiritmt.com/about-camping

OPERATED BY: Spirit Mountain

OPEN: Mid-May–mid-October

SITES: 68 electric (39 with water), 1 double, 10 walk-in, 1 group

EACH SITE HAS: Open tent area, picnic table, fire ring

WHEELCHAIR ACCESS: No designated sites

ASSIGNMENT: Drive-ups and reservations

REGISTRATION: Reservations must be pre-paid; spiritmt.com/about-camping

FACILITIES: Flush toilets, water, showers, RV sanitation station

PARKING: 1 vehicle/site; $5/additional vehicle at site; at trailheads to walk-in sites

FEES: $44/night water and electric, $39/night electric only, $29/night walk-in, $10 cancellation fee, additional fees for multiple tents and RVs (second tent free if for those age 18 and under; $20/additional tent otherwise)

RESTRICTIONS:

PETS: Leashed and attended

QUIET HOURS: 10 p.m.–7 a.m.

FIRES: In fire rings; firewood available at office

ALCOHOL: Permitted

OTHER: This is a private, commercial campground. Check local agencies for current regulations governing activities in the surrounding area. Fireworks and motorized recreational vehicles prohibited; 2-night stay required for holidays and events.

Sites 2, 6, and 7 are open to the road. Site 12 is also open to view from the drive but offers a large space for a tent or two. Site 15 has a couple of good options for a tent site. It is right along the trail that leads out of the campgrounds, across the road to the Timber Twister ride area. Site 16 is another good site with several tent-pitching spots to consider. It is right by the parking lot for those using the lower walk-in sites, F–J. These are back along a trail cut into the heart of the forest and provide a primitive camping setting.

Sites 22, 34, 39, 45, 46, and 48 are large, open tent sites. (Sites 22 and 23 must be booked together.) Site 34 has several good spots to put up a tent. Site 46 is my choice for best site in the campground. It's on a knoll with a scattering of trees surrounding it. While it's easily visible from the road, it sits back and up high enough to command a somewhat lofty perch over its surroundings.

Site 50–68 are average sites, though small in area. Site 56 is rather small but a choice site because it sits back farther into the woods. Likewise, site 68, set back into the trees, provides several places to pitch a tent or two . . . or even three!

Sites 69–72 offer tent spaces in big, open sites. Site 72 is especially long and flanked by tall trees.

Spirit Mountain, despite its proximity to large metropolitan Duluth and the developed ski area, is still situated on the edge of a wilder, more rustic northern Minnesota. Black bears and raccoons are often seen in the campground area. In fact, just prior to my first campout here, a marauding black bear had actually chased a family from its evening meal, commandeering the picnic table for itself. Updated cautionary notices warning of bear activity in the area are posted at the office and shower buildings. Make sure your food is carefully and properly stored—and never in your tent!

Since Spirit Mountain is not a park, the attractions there are man-made—and they are exhilarating. The Timber Twister is an open coaster cart ride down the "mountain" on a rip-roaring 3,200-foot-long track (not an alpine slide) that whips you past trees and sometimes over treetops—with one sweeping swing past an incredible view out over the St. Louis River far below. It's not your normal north-woods camping activity, but it is one heck of a ride. A zip line gives Spirit Mountain campers yet another aerial adrenaline rush to enjoy. Nearby Duluth, the gateway to Lake Superior's fabulous North Shore, is just down the hill from Spirit Mountain and offers great restaurants, a train museum, a freshwater aquarium, a developed waterfront, minigolf, and myriad other attractions.

Spirit Mountain Campground

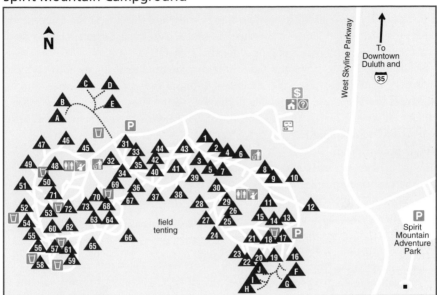

GETTING THERE

From I-35 southwest of Duluth, take Exit 249. Take the south frontage road and follow the signs to the T intersection. Go left (south) on West Skyline Parkway, and continue past the Spirit Mountain main entrance to the campground 0.5 mile farther on the right.

GPS COORDINATES: N46° 42.859' W92° 13.384'

22

⚠ Split Rock Lighthouse State Park Campground

Beauty ★★★★ / Privacy ★★★★★ / Spaciousness ★★★★ / Quiet ★★★ / Security ★★★★★ / Cleanliness ★★★

These beautiful, remote campsites are nestled along the North Shore of Lake Superior with easy access to the historic Split Rock Lighthouse.

Split Rock Lighthouse sites are accessible only by foot, and the closest is a couple hundred feet from the parking lot. However, because it's a rather short, cart-assisted trip to each site *and* this is prime North Shore camping, I decided to list it.

The shoreline here is typical of Lake Superior. Sheer cliffs drop abruptly to the cold, clear waters of the great lake the American Indians called Gitche Gumee. Birch and spruce trees line the shore and extend all the way to the tops of "mountains" more than 1,000 feet tall, formed from ancient lava flows, covered in the sediment of great prehistoric seas, and then sculpted by glacial forces into their present form.

The ruggedness of this shoreline challenged the timber companies harvesting the mature pines that lined these shores. After several ships were lost around the Split Rock area in the early 1900s, a lighthouse and fog signal was contracted in 1909 and operated until 1969. In 1976 the Minnesota Historical Society began operating the site as a tourist attraction and continues to do so today.

The lighthouse attracts visitors, but it's the camping that will keep them there for a night or two. The sites are off a trail that runs along the lake, above and parallel to the shoreline. Four sites are right off the parking lot overlooking the lake, a half dozen more are off the trail that extends up a draw, and the rest are located on either side of a trail that continues north. The farthest campsite is about 2,000 feet from the parking lot.

These are rustic, north-woodsy sites, and each is assigned a large, easy-to-maneuver utility cart. When not hauling gear, the cart can be turned over to serve as a good rain cover for firewood.

Site 1 is off one of the main hiking trails through the park and beyond. It parallels the parking lot, and this site is only a few steps

An iconic North Shore image, the Split Rock Lighthouse near the campground

KEY INFORMATION

ADDRESS: 3755 Split Rock Lighthouse Road, Two Harbors, MN 55616

CONTACT: 218-595-7625, dnr.state.mn.us /state_parks/split_rock_lighthouse

OPERATED BY: Minnesota DNR, Division of Parks and Recreation

OPEN: Year-round (facilities: mid-May–early October)

SITES: 20 cart-in, 2 backpack-in, 2 backpack-in/canoe-in, 1 canoe-in

EACH SITE HAS: Open tent area, picnic table, fire ring

WHEELCHAIR ACCESS: Sites 2 and 3

ASSIGNMENT: Reservations required (same-day reservations available)

REGISTRATION: Reserve at 866-85-PARKS (72757) or tinyurl.com/mnspreservations

FACILITIES: Showers, drinking water, toilet (open mid May–early October); restrooms and water available year-round at the Trail Center

PARKING: Just before trailhead to sites

FEES: $23/night summer season, $17/night off-season, $7 daily permit, $35 annual permit, $8.50 reservation fee

---

RESTRICTIONS:

PETS: On 6-foot leash; attended at all times

QUIET HOURS: 10 p.m.–8 a.m.

FIRES: In fire rings; gathering firewood not permitted; firewood must be purchased from approved vendor

ALCOHOL: Not permitted

OTHER: 6 people/site; closed to visitors 10 p.m.–8 a.m.; fireworks and metal detectors prohibited

---

away, tucked back off the trail and up a small rise, mostly unseen from the trail and any other sites. Sites 2 and 3 (wheelchair accessible) are spread out along the Little Two Harbors Trail, perched like natural balconies high above the tree-covered shoreline below. The sites are exposed to that foot traffic but separated by distance and some vegetation from each other. It's a modest transition from car camping to walk-in camping, a good opportunity to test your wings out on this kind of venture. Site 4 sits on a rock-bordered knoll above the trail and the shower house, with a view of the parking lot and the trail intersection that leads to the rest of the campsites. Up beyond the rock ledge that forms a backdrop for this site is a lofty perch—a great vista of this section of Lake Superior.

Sites 5–10 are off the 8-foot paved pathway that weaves up toward the top of the ridge. The sites are spacious and fairly open but well screened from the other sites. The farther you climb, the closer you are to the North Shore highway—and its traffic noise. At sites along the lake, that sound is muffled by the trees above and drowned out by the wave action below.

That same paved trail drops and weaves downward toward sites 11–20. Site 11 is just off the trail to the left, just past the intersection to sites 5–10. This site shares the same rocky perch mentioned in 5 because it, too, is set back from the edge of a rocky ridge directly above the lake.

About 150 feet farther down the lake trail, you'll find campsites 11–20. These are staggered off the main pathway, half toward the water, half on the slope side. Sites 12, 14, and 15 are all at the base of a 900-foot mound (a trail goes around its base) and are nestled into the dense birch forest that covers this entire area. Site 13 is a short jaunt off toward the water, while sites 16 and 17 also split off to the left from a common trail spur a bit farther down the trail. Sites 18 and 19 are on a point overlooking the lake, and 20 is at the end of the trail. Site 20 sits close to the steep, descending slopes of the mound rising just west of it. This site is a little more than a third of a mile from the parking lot. These campsites will give newcomers an opportunity to experience more primitive, self-sufficient camping. The extra effort is well worth it.

Split Rock Lighthouse State Park offers sightings of deer, moose, black bears (be sure to read the "Camping in Bear Country" information provided at the park), beavers, and more. There are many vistas overlooking the lake, so you should explore hiking options while camping here. You can use the trail system to hike from the campground to the lighthouse site or to connect with the Day Hill Trail that encircles the hill up by the tent sites. There is a spur leading to an overlook on top. Other activities include hiking, beach-combing, and exploring the historic lighthouse. You can also connect with the nearby Gitchi-Gami State Trail that follows along the North Shore.

This campsite has an approach and access that take a little stamina; the reward for this challenge is North Shore scenic Minnesota camping.

Split Rock Lighthouse State Park Campground

GETTING THERE

From Two Harbors take MN 61 about 20 miles north to the park entrance on the right.

GPS COORDINATES: N47° 11.742' W91° 22.777'

23

Temperance River State Park Campground

Beauty ★★★★ / Privacy ★★ / Spaciousness ★★★ / Quiet ★★★ / Security ★★★ / Cleanliness ★★★★

Beautiful waterfalls, rugged river canyons and the stunning shoreline of Lake Superior await campers at this classic North Shore campground.

Temperance River State Park is one of both the North Shore's and Minnesota's classic gems for northern scenic beauty. Its steep, rocky river gorge features several waterfalls and deep potholes. Its picturesque river mouth—with protruding rocks, sandy shorelines and graceful birch trees—that feeds into Lake Superior is a gathering point for photographers, hikers, kayakers, and those just wanting to sit and enjoy the wonders of this incredible geologically enhanced setting. Along with Gooseberry Falls, Temperance River is one of the most popular stopping points along the entire North Shore Scenic Drive. Camping here is an added bonus.

The campgrounds are laid out in two loops, Upper and Lower, and are situated on both sides of the Temperance River gorge, and each has its own entrance off the North Shore Scenic Drive/MN 61.

The Upper Campground consists of three essentially nondescript but appealing loops, each laid out amid a forest of mostly northern evergreens and mixed aspen/birch. The understory offers a lush visual buffer between the campsites. Campsites 1–20 all share the

The rocky point at the mouth of the Temperance River in the Lower Campground

KEY INFORMATION

ADDRESS: 7620 W. MN 61, Schroeder, MN 55613

CONTACT: 218-663-3100, dnr.state.mn.us /state_parks/temperance_river (winter: Tettegouche State Park: 218-353-8800)

OPERATED BY: Minnesota DNR, Division of Parks and Recreation

OPEN: Upper Campground: late March–late December (water/showers: early May–late October); Lower Campground: mid-April–mid-November (water/showers: early May–late October)

SITES: 53 (17 with electric), 6 cart-in

EACH SITE HAS: Tent pad area, picnic table, fire ring

WHEELCHAIR ACCESS: No designated sites; showers and flush toilets accessible

ASSIGNMENT: Reservations required (same-day reservations available)

REGISTRATION: Reserve at 866-85-PARKS (72757) or tinyurl.com/mnspreservations

FACILITIES: Restrooms (flush toilets in Upper Campground; vault toilets in Lower), showers (in Upper), water, boat ramp

PARKING: 1 vehicle/site

FEES: $23/night summer season, $17/night off-season, $31/night electric sites, $7 daily permit, $35 annual permit, $8.50 reservation fee

---

RESTRICTIONS:

PETS: On 6-foot leash; attended at all times

QUIET HOURS: 10 p.m.–8 a.m.

FIRES: In fire rings; gathering firewood not permitted; firewood must be purchased from approved vendor

ALCOHOL: Not permitted

OTHER: 1 tent/site; 6 people/site; closed to visitors 10 p.m.–8 a.m.; fireworks and metal detectors prohibited

---

same characteristics: each is fairly small and each is very close to the road, providing very little privacy from those driving by. Sites 5, 12, and 13 offer better views toward the lake. Sites 20–38 appear to be more spread out along the roadway but still have short driveways and exposed campsites. Sites 26 and 28 offer the best perspectives for enjoying a view of the lake through the trees. In general, these sites are pleasantly laid out, just small and not set back very far into the cover of the understory from the campground road.

The entrance to the Lower Campground is at the end of the turnout parking lot immediately before crossing over the Temperance River from the south. It could be easily missed as one approaches the hub of activity, as pedestrians park and walk to enjoy the incredible views of the river gorge from the highway bridge. However, once you enter this campground area you may quickly understand why it was my preferred section for camping. The campsites are approached by a drive right along the shoreline that provides an inviting vista out to the southern horizon of Lake Superior.

A grassy strip between the roadway and the shoreline is the campground's picnic area. It also parallels a sandy beach—ideal for launching kayaks. The rocky walls of the mouth of the Temperance River provide an inspiring backdrop where the river empties into the lake.

Campsites 40–44 are right alongside the road, across from the open shoreline, making them totally exposed to both campground foot and vehicle traffic and totally unprotected against any weather approaching off the lake. These are small sites, especially well suited for canoeists and kayakers who simply need a land base to pitch a tent and regroup, practically at the water's edge. The rest of the sites are very close to the road as well and rank low on the privacy scale. Sites 52 and 55 are only slightly more hidden by understory. Several footpaths that lead to the lake cut through the campground at several points between the campsites. Visitors can enjoy the Temperance River from several vantage points accessible by hiking trails along both sides of the gorge; from the walkway along the bridge over the gorge; or from access trails in each of the two campgrounds. Trails along the river are segments of the Superior Hiking Trail that runs along the entire North Shore. Coupled with those and other hiking options, campers can fish for trout stocked in the Temperance River. As part of a segment of the Lake Superior Water Trail, you can enjoy paddling along the shoreline of the greatest of the Great Lakes. There is also a motorboat access about a mile south in the town of Schroeder.

The Temperance River is among a half dozen major waterfall attractions along the North Shore. At about the midpoint between Duluth and the Canadian border, its choice location puts it at less than an hour's drive from all the key natural and historic features along the famous North Shore Drive.

Temperance River State Park Campground

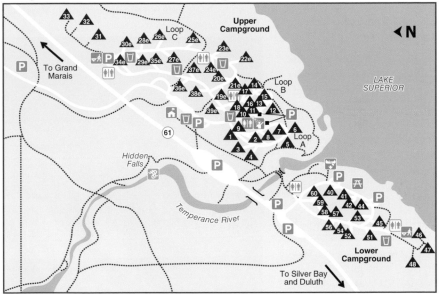

GETTING THERE

From the intersection of MN 1 and MN 61 in Illgen City, go north 21 miles on MN 61 to the park entrance on the right. From the intersection of CR 2 and MN 61 in Tofte, go south 2.3 miles on MN 61 to the park entrance on the left.

GPS COORDINATES:
LOWER CAMPGROUND: N47° 33.223' W90° 52.475'
UPPER CAMPGROUND: N47° 33.295' W90° 52.331'

24

Tettegouche State Park Campground

Beauty ★★★★ / Privacy ★★★★★ / Spaciousness ★★★★★ / Quiet ★★★★ / Security ★★★ / Cleanliness ★★★★

Take your pick, from a Lake Superior shoreline, numerous rapids, cascades, and the state's tallest waterfall (within the state's borders) to rugged, mountainlike terrain and northern hardwood forests.

Tettegouche State Park is one of my favorites. The rivers, waterfalls (including High Falls, the tallest in the state), and rapids are indescribable, and the hiking is some of the best in the region—what's not to like?

I remember this area from many years ago, before it was called Tettegouche. I had come here from Minneapolis to hike and enjoy the incredible waterfalls and cascading rivers. I don't remember camping being an option way back then, so the opportunity to review this park was a real treat for me.

Like most properties converted to parks, this one has its roots in Minnesota's timber industry. Once the timber was harvested, the lumber company sold the area to a group of Duluth businessmen—the Tettegouche Club—to be used as a fishing retreat. It changed hands a number of times until it became a park in 1979.

Outflows of lava (along a rift line that stretches all the way to Kansas), layers of seabed sediment, and scouring by several glacial periods all helped create the park we enjoy today. The drainage patterns of this part of the North Shore created the numerous waterfalls and cascades for which this and other parks in the area are known.

Whitetail deer, snowshoe hares, and 140 species of birds make up the cast of fauna common to this area. The gleaming trunks of aspen and birch by the big lake are replaced by the upland hardwoods of sugar maple, yellow birch, basswood,

photographed by Lisa A. Crayford

Baptism Falls at Tettegouche

KEY INFORMATION

ADDRESS: 5702 MN 61, East Silver Bay, MN 55614

CONTACT: 218-353-8800, dnr.state.mn.us /state_parks/tettegouche

OPERATED BY: Minnesota DNR, Division of Parks and Recreation

OPEN: Year-round

SITES: 27 (20 with electric), 6 walk-in, 14 cart-in, 5 backpack-in, 1 cabin, 4 walk-in cabins, 2 group

EACH SITE HAS: Open tent area, picnic table, fire ring

WHEELCHAIR ACCESS: No designated sites

ASSIGNMENT: Reservations required (same-day reservations available)

REGISTRATION: Reserve at 866-85-PARKS (72757) or tinyurl.com/mnspreservations

FACILITIES: Restroom, showers, water, boat ramp

PARKING: 1 vehicle/site (2 vehicles/site with permission)

FEES: $23/night summer season, $31/night electric sites, $7 daily permit, $35 annual permit, $8.50 reservation fee

---

RESTRICTIONS:

PETS: On 6-foot leash; attended at all times

QUIET HOURS: 10 p.m.–8 a.m.

FIRES: In fire rings; gathering firewood not permitted; firewood must be purchased from approved vendor

ALCOHOL: Not permitted

OTHER: 1 tent/site; 6 people/site; closed to visitors 10 p.m.–8 a.m.; fireworks and metal detectors prohibited

and spruce as that mature forest evolves throughout the inland lake country. Lone pines scattered frequently throughout the park tower above this forest canopy.

The drive-in campground offers some fantastic sites, including a walk-in campsite that is among my favorites. Sites 1–5 are typical, having all the standard features. They are well screened but small and fairly close to the road compared to others in this area.

The walk-in sites, 6–8, are easily accessible from the small parking area located at the head of the trail leading to the sites. Site 6 sits in a stand of old-growth birch and is very private. Site 7 is located on a slight rise in the forest floor, and 8 is on top of a modest ridge with a growing understory of aspen and balsam fir; these two sites are separated by about 150 feet.

Site 9 is small and tidy. Sites 10–16 are basic sites within a dense understory. Sites 13 and 14 are partially surrounded by a grove of cedars. Site 15 sits on the edge of a ridge, and 16 sits in a stand of aspen and fir—a quaint camping spot. Sites on either side of the road throughout this loop are all pleasant and inviting.

Site 18 is probably the smallest in the loop. A trail heads off to the river, leading down the slope from the road at a point between sites 17 and 20. Site 21 is long and narrow—not much tent space there.

Sites 24 and 25 are walk-in sites, requiring a short hike from the parking area across the road. Site 25 is a spot to cherish. It's not anywhere near the water but is so private and spacious that it's worth extra effort to secure it. Both sites are far enough off the road to give them a true backcountry feel. They are surrounded by clusters of birch, boulders, and a quiet forest. Site 25 has a sprinkling of cedar trees. It is a very private site, guarded by a towering white pine.

A rock outcrop as the loop starts to circle back on itself is an impressive backdrop to sites 26 and 27. The next few sites are standard and noticeably exposed compared to earlier sites in the loop. The remaining sites vary in size and shape but still retain the character of this campground.

One can imagine these hills aglow in the fall when all the birch and aspen leaves turn their brilliant yellow. Add the reds and oranges of the other hardwoods, and you can count on excellent fall color throughout this area.

It's safe to say that if you had only one chance to experience a drive-in tent-camping experience along the North Shore, Tettegouche State Park would be a most gratifying and fulfilling choice.

Tettegouche State Park Campground

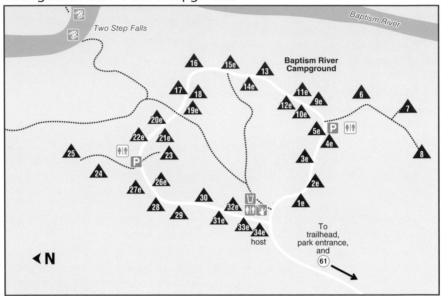

GETTING THERE

From Silver Bay go 4.5 miles north on MN 61 to the park entrance on the right.

GPS COORDINATES: N47° 20.731' W91° 12.585'

25

⛺ Zippel Bay State Park Campgrounds

Beauty ★★★ / Privacy ★★★ / Spaciousness ★★★ / Quiet ★★★ / Security ★★★ / Cleanliness ★★★★

This fisherman's park is set in a dense stand of picturesque birch trees on the southern shore of Lake of the Woods.

This park took me completely by surprise! I am no stranger to northern Minnesota—one of my most enjoyable camping trips ever was on a small island on the Lake of the Woods—but I was not prepared for Zippel Bay State Park.

Located on the southern shore of Lake of the Woods, this is Minnesota's northernmost state park. It is situated along a 2-mile stretch of beach in a birch and jack pine forest overlooking the oceanic vastness of Lake of the Woods. The lake itself is an awesome body of water, more than 1,600 square miles with almost 10 times as many islands throughout its waterways. I was at Zippel about a week after the full flush of fall colors. Even then, the golden canopy of birch leaves was almost blinding. Brilliant golden-yellow leaves at the end of long, limber, powdery-white tree trunks played beautifully against the blue sky overhead. Fantastic fall coloration greeted me throughout the park. The birch stands in some areas are so thick and so tightly grown, their long gleaming white trunks so close together, that I made an entry in my notebook: "I feel like a flea on the back of a white-haired dog!" Amid this wash of whites and yellows, the campgrounds are laid out.

Zippel Bay has four campgrounds: Lady's-Slipper, Birch, Ridge, and Angler's. No sites have electricity.

Lady's-Slipper has the fewest sites, all off one long driveway ending in a cul-de-sac. The 11 sites alternate on each side of the road. They are nestled into the woods, but the lack of understory and space between them does not afford much privacy.

As you might expect, Birch Campground is anchored in a thick sea of birch trees. The campground is at the end of a 200-yard spur off the main road. Sites 2–17 are fairly close

Lake of the Woods shoreline near the campground

photographed by Joe Henry/Lake of the Woods Tourism

KEY INFORMATION

ADDRESS: 3684 54th Ave. NW, Williams, MN 56686

CONTACT: 218-783-6252, dnr.state.mn.us /state_parks/zippel_bay (Big Bog State Recreation Area: 218-647-8592)

OPERATED BY: Minnesota DNR, Division of Parks and Recreation

OPEN: April–October (facilities: May–early October)

SITES: 57, 1 group

EACH SITE HAS: Open tent area, picnic table, fire ring

WHEELCHAIR ACCESS: No designated sites, but all should provide acceptable access

ASSIGNMENT: Reservations required (same-day reservations available)

REGISTRATION: Reserve at 866-85-PARKS (72757) or tinyurl.com/mnspreservations

FACILITIES: Drinking water, vault toilets, RV sanitation station, showers

PARKING: 1 vehicle/site (2 vehicles/site with permission); on right just before entrance

FEES: $23/night summer season, $17/night off-season, $7 daily permit, $35 annual permit, $8.50 reservation fee

---

RESTRICTIONS:

PETS: On 6-foot leash; attended at all times

QUIET HOURS: 10 p.m.–8 a.m.

FIRES: In fire rings; gathering firewood not permitted; firewood must be purchased from approved vendor

ALCOHOL: Not permitted

OTHER: 6 people/site; closed to visitors 10 p.m.–8 a.m.; fireworks and metal detectors prohibited

---

together. The sites begin to spread out a bit more at 18. All the sites in Birch, Ridge, and Angler's are outside the camping road loop, so there are no sites directly or alternately across from each other. Sites at the tip of the loop are the most private and spacious.

Ridge is probably the best campground of the four as far as space between sites and general sense of privacy. It sits at the end of a long, narrow lane—farther than depicted on the park map. Sites on the northern and southern edges of the loop (29–32 and 37–40) are a bit farther apart.

Angler's Campground is, as the name implies, a convenient campsite for those heavily into boat fishing. It is closest to the marina area, and each site is large enough to accommodate a large tent, vehicles, and presumably boat trailers. There is not much of an understory at Angler's, but the birch and interspersed jack pine give it a wonderful, woodsy setting.

Besides the dominance of birch trees throughout the park, expect to see clusters of aspen inland (those at Zippel Bay have very whitish bark), gradually changing to birch closer to the lake. There are patches of evergreens in the park, too, mostly balsam fir, in the area around Angler's Campground. Jack pines are scattered about as well, but it's clearly the white paper birches that draw the eye.

The park's list of natural amenities is mighty impressive. There are four species of lady's slipper orchids and several other orchid species. Wild berries (blue-, June-, cran-, and straw-) flourish in June and July, as do mushrooms, pin cherries, and chokecherries.

Wildlife-viewing possibilities abound as well: coyote, black bear, mink, fisher, otter, and even a rare pine marten. Even timber wolves are seen or heard in the park. Deer and an occasional moose are seen as well.

Birding is a popular activity too, as many species are attracted to the great expanse of water and its miles of shoreline. White pelicans, double-crested cormorants, several gull varieties, and four species of terns are common along the park's shoreline. Less common sandhill cranes frequent a marsh just north of Zippel Bay. You might even see the rare threatened piping plover. You might see spruce grouse throughout the campgrounds as well.

Other recreational amenities include fishing, boating access from the public boat harbor, a launching ramp and dock, picnic and fish-cleaning areas, and a hiking trail. Canoe rentals may be available on summer weekends.

Historically, this park was home to several American Indian tribes. French explorers scouted out the area in the early 1700s. By the late 1880s a small fishing village was established by the park's namesake, William M. Zippel.

The big draw of Zippel Bay is, of course, Lake of the Woods—a most impressive body of water. Fishing for walleye is the most popular activity on the lake (with a sauger or two taken, and even a sturgeon), with beachcombing and swimming at the park a close second and third. Still, in my view, the park is worth a camping outing for the birch forests alone.

Zippel Bay State Park Campgrounds

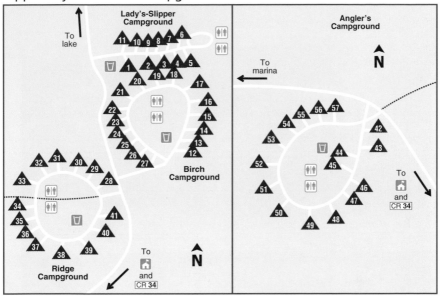

GETTING THERE

From Williams head north on Wilderness Avenue/CR 2. Go 5.3 miles, and turn right (east) onto CR 8. In 5.8 miles turn left (north) onto CR 34/54th Avenue NW. Go 1.25 miles to the park entrance, and another 0.75 mile to the campground road on the right.

From the west end of Baudette, take MN 172 north 10.5 miles to CR 8. Turn left (west) onto CR 8, and go 6 miles to CR 34/54th Avenue NW. Turn right (north), go 1.25 miles to the park entrance, and travel another 0.75 mile to the campground road on the right.

GPS COORDINATES: N48° 51.447' W94° 50.202'

CENTRAL MINNESOTA

Rapids on the Snake River—a state water trail (see page 118)

26

Ann Lake Campground

Beauty ★★★ / Privacy ★★★ / Spaciousness ★★★ / Quiet ★★★ / Security ★★★ / Cleanliness ★★★

Ann Lake features pine- and oak-covered sand dunes laced with rambling trails.

Rarely would I recommend camping in an area shared by horseback riding, but Ann Lake, while attracting both horseback riders and snowmobilers, is also a pretty darn good place to camp and hike. Besides, those other two popular activities are not allowed in the camping area, which is designated on maps as the Bob Dunn Recreation Area.

State forests offer an alternative way of enjoying and appreciating the outdoors; they are less structured and less developed, but they are by no means less appealing. You will be ahead of the game if you are easily entertained by nature itself. A state forest setting may not always be as spectacular as a state park or have nearly the geological, historical, or other amenities that distinguish parks from the outdoors in general. Yet state forest campgrounds are a pleasant way to enjoy the forest for what it is—whether you are passing through on an overnight or this is your destination for a week's stay under the stars.

What I especially like about the state forest campgrounds is that they are usually located off the main arteries of highways and scenic routes and often are stuck in the middle of nowhere—even within the forest itself. They consist of basic campsites cut out of the forest and developed to the extent that there is a tent site, a picnic table, a fire ring, a pit toilet, and few other amenities. "Wait a minute," you are probably saying. "That's as much as a state park offers?" Yes, indeed, basic sites in a more utilitarian setting—but wonderful camping just the same.

That said, here's what's special about Ann Lake: First of all, it is situated within Sand Dunes State Forest. This area used to be part of the expansive prairie system that covered the western and southwestern parts of Minnesota. However, the sandy soils were not conducive to pioneer farming methods, and those who homesteaded the region fought

Campsite in the oak forests of Ann Lake

courtesy of the Minnesota Department of Natural Resources

KEY INFORMATION

ADDRESS: North Sand Dunes Forest Road, 0.8 mile south of 168th Street, Big Lake, MN 55309

CONTACT: 763-878-2325, dnr.state.mn.us /state_forests/facilities/cmp00046

OPERATED BY: Sand Dunes State Forest (managed by Lake Maria State Park)

OPEN: Early to mid-April–October

SITES: 30 drive-in, 6 walk-in, 4 walk-in group

EACH SITE HAS: Open tent area, picnic table, fire ring

WHEELCHAIR ACCESS: Sites 7 and 24

ASSIGNMENT: First come, first served; reservations for group sites

REGISTRATION: Fee box

FACILITIES: Vault toilets, water, boat ramp nearby

PARKING: 2 vehicles/site; at both ends of the trail loop into the walk-in sites; parking area for group sites

FEES: $14/night, $50/night group site

RESTRICTIONS:

PETS: On leash

QUIET HOURS: 10 p.m.–8 a.m.

FIRES: In fire rings; gathering downed and dead firewood permitted; firewood must be purchased from approved vendor

ALCOHOL: Not permitted

OTHER: 8 people/site; hunting and firearms only in posted areas; camping possible in undeveloped areas

---

long and hard to grow crops here. During the Great Depression, it was determined that the area's economy could be better established if trees were planted in the sandy soil, and since the early 1940s, more than 2,400 acres of tree plantations have been established here. Many of the hiking trails throughout the Bob Dunn Recreation Area pass through these blocks of plantings. The forests in and around Ann Lake were eventually built up to cover more than 17 square miles, featuring northern pines as well as other species (predominantly oak) that found the area suitable for growth.

You can't help but notice the stands of red pine and oak varieties within the campground. Each site offers a spacious setting under a bur oak canopy. Sites 3–12 are set into a hilly, oak-forested area with an ample understory that affords a bit of privacy and quietness. (Site 7 is wheelchair accessible.) Within this loop, sites 8–12 are situated on slightly higher ground; though these sites may provide less privacy, they have a more commanding view and presence than others within the campground's first loop.

The next few sites (13 is the host site), 14–21, are much closer together but are laid out to provide plenty of room within each site's immediate area. Generally the sites are well spread out among the hills and the turns of the campground road to create individual settings—either on knolls or in openings scattered throughout the woods. The entire lower campground loop offers a thick understory, giving each site a sense of isolation from the rest. In the next cluster of campsites, site 24 is also wheelchair accessible.

The lower end of the 2-mile nature trail can be accessed at the entrance to the campground. A short trail takes hikers to a fork that lets them access the Red Loop in either direction for a full round of hiking through pine plantations and stands of oaks and along ridgelines atop the dunes.

The walk-in sites are located at the end of the main campground loop. As in all the other areas covered in this book, the walk-in sites are usually my favorite picks. I love the solitude and the basic amenities. These sites are nestled among the knolls or dunes of the park. Sites 35 and 36 overlook Ann Lake.

The best campsites are in the group camp area just below the fire tower and immediately above the lake. It's a beautiful setting in the shadow of the old fire tower and a planting of white pines started in 1978. There is a spur from the main trail system that leads into this camping area. It connects with the Orange Loop on the trail system, which then intersects with other loops in the network. Park activities and amenities also include horseback riding, a network of snowmobile and hiking trails, swimming, and a boat access ramp. I found the group site to be the most beautiful in the park. Gather up a half dozen or so of those you'd most like to camp with, and make a reservation for the group site—I doubt you'll be disappointed.

Note: If you enjoy bird-watching, the northern section of the Sherburne National Wildlife Refuge is a mere 6-mile drive north of Ann Lake. It features a 7-mile wildlife drive through grasslands, along a series of drainage gates and through controlled sloughs for fantastic waterfowl and shorebird watching. The loop is a great hiking trail, too. There are also several opportunities to see nesting bald eagles.

Ann Lake Campground

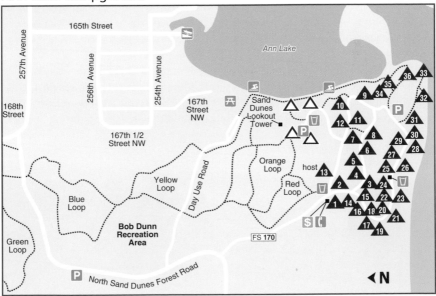

GETTING THERE

From Zimmerman take CR 4 west 5 miles, then turn left (south) onto 168th Street. After 0.5 mile, where 168th Street turns east, turn west (right) onto North Sand Dunes Forest Road for 0.8 mile. Turn left onto FS 170, and go southeast 0.3 mile to the fee station at the campground.

GPS COORDINATES: N45° 25.546' W93° 41.814'

27

Banning State Park Campground

Beauty ★★ / Privacy ★★ / Spaciousness ★★★ / Quiet ★★★ / Security ★★★ / Cleanliness ★★★

Geological offerings abound in this park dominated by the Kettle River—it's truly a treasure chest of natural amenities.

This park is teeming with amenities, such as a waterfall, sets of rapids, exposed bedrock, and all the other natural features of the great northern Minnesota woods. Its geological features alone make it a park worth visiting.

Banning State Park is composed of more than 6,200 acres adjacent to the Kettle River, one of Minnesota's Wild and Scenic Rivers. Cutting through the bedrock that underlies most of Minnesota and is exposed throughout so much of the north country, Banning's Kettle River has carved out several sets of rapids on its course through the park. If you are not a river runner, you can at least enjoy an afternoon of watching the more courageous river rats shooting these disturbances.

One section of the river, Hell's Gate, is a graphic example of the geological forces that have sculpted this park. After carving a trough through 100 feet of Precambrian sandstone, the Kettle River carved sheer, 40-foot cliffs out of the bedrock to create this canyon. More fanciful geological formations within the park include the kettles, the sandstone quarry, and Wolf Creek Falls.

This is a birder's park, featuring more than 184 species that either visit or migrate through. Other wildlife abounds, offering visitors a long list of critters to see during a visit.

Human influences are seen mostly in the aspen and birch trees that dominate the forest. These are what came in to replace all the white and red pine harvested during Minnesota's

Big Spring Falls on the Kettle River

photographed by Lisa A. Crayford

KEY INFORMATION

ADDRESS: 61101 Banning Park Road, Sandstone, MN 55072

CONTACT: 320-245-2668, dnr.state.mn.us/state_parks/banning

OPERATED BY: Minnesota DNR, Division of Parks and Recreation

OPEN: April–mid-November (facilities: early May–early October)

SITES: 33 drive-in (11 with electric), 5 canoe-in, 1 camper cabin

EACH SITE HAS: Open tent area (some sites with tent pads), picnic table, fire ring

WHEELCHAIR ACCESS: Site 2 (not officially ADA) and camper cabin

ASSIGNMENT: Reservations required (same-day reservations available)

REGISTRATION: Reserve at 866-85-PARKS (72757) or tinyurl.com/mnspreservations

FACILITIES: Restroom, showers, recycling center, electric sites, water

PARKING: 1 vehicle/site (2 vehicles/site with permission); past entrance to campground loop

FEES: $23/night, $17/night off-season, $31/night electric sites, $25/night electric sites off-season, $7 daily permit, $35 annual permit, $8.50 reservation fee

RESTRICTIONS:

PETS: On 6-foot leash; attended at all times

QUIET HOURS: 10 p.m.–8 a.m.

FIRES: In fire rings; gathering firewood not permitted; firewood must be purchased from approved vendor

ALCOHOL: Not permitted

OTHER: 6 people/site; closed to visitors 10 p.m.–8 a.m.; fireworks and metal detectors prohibited

---

logging blitz. A few towering pines and an understory that includes younger spruce indicate that the forest is slowly maturing.

This area was devastated by the Great Hinckley Fire of 1894. The town of Banning, named after the president of the local railroad, saw its population decline after several more forest fires in the area and was abandoned by 1912.

Camping here is confined to one three-section loop located in the center of the long, narrow, north–south–oriented park. Most of the trail systems pass between the camping area and the river just east of the campground.

The first section of the loop contains eight sites, five of which include electricity and so will attract the RVs and appliance-dependent campers. It's a small lane with red pine, aspen, and paper birch.

Almost all of the nonelectric campsites have a tent pad made of wood chips. Sites 1–3 are surrounded by a good screening from the abundant understory but are pretty basic otherwise. Site 2 is wheelchair accessible (thought it's not officially ADA compliant).

Sites 9–17 are off staggered driveways, which means a modest degree of privacy as far as looking across the road to another site. However, these sites are fairly well exposed to the road down the driveway. A thick understory increases privacy and probably helps muffle the sound a bit. Sites 10, 12, and 13 offer electrical hookups.

The last section of the loop contains sites 18–34; these are better for optimum tent-camping enjoyment. The inner sites, 20, 22, and 24, are also electrically enhanced. This section is within a stand of older aspens, and many sites have a dense understory to promote privacy and quiet.

Site 18 has a long driveway off the main loop and backs up to the forest; it is very isolated and private. Site 19, also on the outer edge of the loop, is nestled into that dense understory. Actually, even those sites within the loop are adequately spaced to offer a sense of privacy. Site 23, on the other hand, is too open for my liking. Sites 24 and 25 are good sites size-wise but are also more open than the former sites in this loop. There is also one rental cabin in the park, located at site 31. Site 32, although in the inner loop, is very big but lacks understory.

This area features stands of aspens intermixed with evergreens (mostly spruce and balsam fir), creating a pleasant contrast of colors that is certainly heightened during fall when the deep green of the spruce is the backdrop for the brilliant gold of the aspens.

Banning State Park's forest floor is covered with barrel-size boulders—remnants of the tremendous geological influences on this region. For those who enjoy learning about and seeing the evidence of Minnesota's rich geological history, Banning should be just the spot. Birders and hikers will be equally rewarded. Other popular activities include skiing, canoeing, kayaking (some challenging whitewater runs too!), and fishing.

Banning State Park Campground

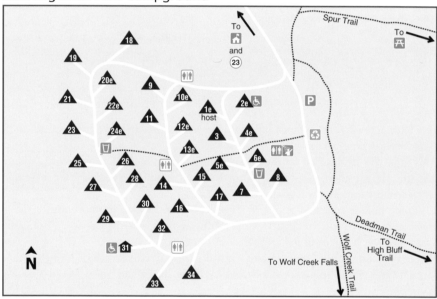

GETTING THERE

From Sandstone go north 3 miles on MN 23, then turn right to stay on MN 23 another 1 mile to the campground entrance. Or take I-35 to Exit 195, and head east on MN 23 0.3 mile to the park entrance on the right.

GPS COORDINATES: N46° 9.347' W92° 51.273'

28

Bunker Hills Campground: RUSTIC LOOP

Beauty ★★★ / Privacy ★★★★ / Spaciousness ★★★★ / Quiet ★★★ / Security ★★★★ / Cleanliness ★★★★

This oak-forest setting is just minutes north of downtown Minneapolis and has a true country-camping atmosphere.

Bunker Hills Regional Park lies just beyond the last of the suburbs of the metropolitan Twin Cities, north side (including the Anoka area), and the ever-expanding open country to the north. The park is a pocket of sandy hills, oak forests, and a small lake that has been developed into one of the major regional parks in Anoka County and is probably more renowned for its incredible water park, which draws swimmers, waders, and splashers from all around the seven-county metro area. I doubt many people even realize it has a campground—and a choice one at that!

Bunker Hills Campground is within the regional park and as such is part of its complex of recreational activities. Hiking trails wind through the campground and wooded areas; riding stables and a golf course are also located within the park. The programs and amenities are all designed for and openly encourage full family participation and enjoyment.

There is a wonderful walking/biking trail that works its way through the Bunker Hills complex. It curves through the oaks and up and over swales along its wooded course. The total trail is about 5 miles long and at several points intersects with spurs that offer shortcuts back to the campgrounds or to some of the key recreational sections of the park (the water park, for example). Birders will be kept busy with all the park's songbirds.

There are three campground loops at Bunker Hills, two completely serviced with hookups for RVs (sites 13 and 14 are wheelchair-accessible campsites) and one rustic loop for tent camping. The Rustic Loop features 19 campsites and 2 cabins spread out among a cluster of oaks and pines, offering large sites with optimum privacy in most cases. Because this

is a continuation of the campground numbering system that includes the RV side, the Rustic Loop begins at site 25, which is a fairly exposed site backed by red pines and oaks. Likewise, site 26 is exposed and adjacent to a small playground area. The road through the campground twists through a forest of oak trees, both mature trees that form the canopy overhead and saplings that make up the understory. There are a few aspens intermixed—like those scattered around site 27, which sits on a rise above the roadway.

courtesy of Anoka County Parks

Tent site in the Rustic Loop

KEY INFORMATION

ADDRESS: 13101 County Parkway B, Coon Rapids, MN 55433

CONTACT: 763-324-3330 (seasonal), anokacounty.us/910/camping

OPERATED BY: Anoka County Parks

OPEN: May–mid-October

SITES: 13 rustic, 8 (50-amp) electric/water, 2 camper cabins, 1 group (48 full hookup in two other loops)

EACH SITE HAS: Open tent area, picnic table, fire ring

WHEELCHAIR ACCESS: Sites 13 and 14, in the first RV loop

ASSIGNMENT: First come, first served, unless reserved; all reservable

REGISTRATION: At campground office; reserve sites at 763-324-3330

FACILITIES: Restrooms, showers, water

PARKING: 2 vehicles/site (except sites 34A–34D, which share a parking spur); no parking on grass; vehicles must have an Anoka, Washington, or Carver County permit

FEES: $20 rustic sites, $32 (50-amp) sites with water, $55/night camper cabins, $6 daily permit, $30 annual permit, $8 reservation fee

---

RESTRICTIONS:

PETS: On leash and attended; no more than 2 pets/site

QUIET HOURS: 10 p.m.–8 a.m.

FIRES: In fire rings; gathering firewood not permitted; firewood must be purchased from visitor center

ALCOHOL: Beer only (no glass allowed)

OTHER: 2 tents/site; 6 people/site; closed to visitors 10 p.m.–8 a.m.; fireworks prohibited

Site 28 is open and grassy, and the site directly across the road, 29, sits in a grove of trees. Both are screened by a dense understory. Site 30 is off the road to the right in a little pocket of large oaks all by itself. The road continues through the trees, but off to the right you'll get a glimpse of the water park area. In the summer, expect to hear it way before you see it.

Sites 31–33 are all exposed to the road but are within defined open areas, making them uncrowded places to pitch a tent. Large, looming oak trees stand sentinel over these sites.

Site 34 is divided into four sites, A, B, C, and D, at the end of a spur off the main campground road. Each site has a short access trail leading to it before it opens into a clearing in the woods. These shaded sites, off the main trail, are especially pleasant.

Site 35 sits on a grassy knoll surrounded by gnarly oak trees. Site 36 is exposed to the road a bit more than others but is back far enough in the trees to provide a private, grassy area for pitching a tent or two. Sites 37 and 38 are camper cabins; site 39 is near a hiking trail intersection.

Sites 40–44 seem the least private, most exposed sites in the park, mainly because the entrance road to the campground runs behind them (except for site 42) and can be seen through the trees.

Bunker Hills Campground is a cross between the nearby north woods and the oak savannas of south-central and eastern Minnesota. It has charm, class, and lots of spacious campsites that put many state park campgrounds to shame. Its proximity to the Twin Cities makes it a good pick for weekend camping trips when you just need to get out of the house for a while. Be sure to take the Rustic Loop; otherwise you'll be in the ring of wagons at the RV campground. Campers can enjoy hiking, swimming, water park activities, horseback riding, and golf.

Bunker Hills Campground: Rustic Loop

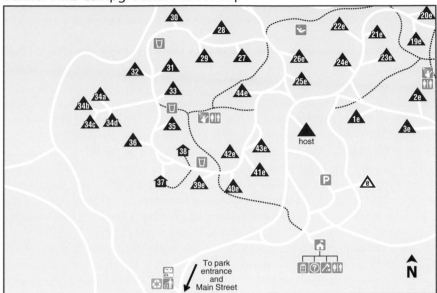

GETTING THERE

From Minneapolis take I-35W north to Exit 30 for US 10; go west on US 10 for 2.2 miles to MN 65 (Central Avenue NE). At MN 65 take a right (north) and go 5.8 miles to Bunker Lake Boulevard NW. Turn left (west) and go 2.7 miles to the entrance. Turn left (south) into the park. From Saint Paul take I-35E north to I-694 W. Go west on I-694 about 6 miles to I-35W North, and then follow the directions above.

GPS COORDINATES: N45° 12.572' W93° 16.685'

29

Glendalough State Park Campground

Beauty ★★★ / Privacy ★★★ / Spaciousness ★★★★ / Quiet ★★★★ / Security ★★★★★ / Cleanliness ★★★★

A short walk leads to expansive, wooded campsites above a tranquil lake offering fishing and canoeing.

As one of only a couple of walk-in/cart-in campgrounds in this guide, Glendalough offers pleasant sites, all quite easily accessible via a short walk from the parking lot. And like the others, it even provides a wheelchair-accessible campsite close to the parking lot.

Developed as a park from land that had once been both a corporate retreat and a game farm, Glendalough's key natural features include a thousand acres of water among several lakes, including the crystal-clear Annie Battle Lake. Designated as a heritage fishery, this lake is maintained and managed in a style referred to as a primitive fishing theme—special regulations prohibit motorized boating while enhancing sportfishing options through management and monitoring. It's a wonderful body of water for paddlers and anglers.

The flora and fauna here are characteristic of this region of Minnesota that is along the transitional zone between the hardwood forests of the east and the prairie landscapes of the west. A section of the lake's shoreline represents one of very few tracts of undeveloped shoreline in western Minnesota.

The campsite is arranged in a long loop along the west side of Annie Battle Lake. A well-defined pathway leads from the service area at the parking lot down through the 22 campsites staggered throughout the predominantly maple and oak hardwood forest. Sites here are equipped with food-storage boxes that can also serve as benchlike seating or a work surface near the picnic table.

An open, spacious site

KEY INFORMATION

ADDRESS: 25287 Whitetail Lane, Battle Lake, MN 56515

CONTACT: 218-864-0110, dnr.state.mn.us /state_parks/glendalough

OPERATED BY: Minnesota DNR, Division of Parks and Recreation

OPEN: Year-round (water/showers: mid-May–early October)

SITES: 22 cart-in, 3 canoe-in (or bike-in, backpack-in, bike-in, or sled-in), 4 camper cabins, 2 yurts, 1 group

EACH SITE HAS: Open tent area, picnic table, fire ring, some sites with food-storage boxes

WHEELCHAIR ACCESS: Site 2 and cabin 3

ASSIGNMENT: All reservable

REGISTRATION: Reserve at 866-85-PARKS (72757) or tinyurl.com/mnspreservations

FACILITIES: Restrooms and water open year-round at Trail Center (0.75 mile away from cart-in campground); water and showers at campgrounds seasonal; all wheelchair accessible; vault toilet at cart-in campground

PARKING: Large parking area adjacent to entrance to cart-in campground

FEES: $21/night, $17/night off-season, $7 daily permit, $35 annual permit, $8.50 reservation fee

---

RESTRICTIONS:

PETS: On 6-foot leash; attended at all times

QUIET HOURS: 10 p.m.–8 a.m.

FIRES: In fire rings; gathering firewood not permitted; firewood must be purchased from approved vendor

ALCOHOL: Not permitted

OTHER: 6 people/site; closed to visitors 10 p.m.–8 a.m.; fireworks and metal detectors prohibited; nonmotorized boats only on Annie Battle Lake

Sites 1 and 2 are immediately to the left and right, respectively, of the intersection of the broad pathway between the restrooms/kiosk complex and the campground loop. Site 2 is the campground's only designated wheelchair-accessible site. Sites 4, 5, and 7 are within an open understory and very spacious. Sites 3 and 6 are camper cabins, and cabin 3 is wheelchair accessible. Site 8 is small compared to most others in the campground.

Site 9 is big and open, but its clear view over to site 18 makes it perhaps less private than others. Sites 10 and 12 are the park's two other camper-cabin sites. Site 11 is situated across from a cabin and slopes slightly away from the otherwise broad and level pathway. Sites 13 and 14 are at the southern end of the campground loop—each large, open sites. Campers at site 14, which is outside the loop, enjoy an open view of a prairie hillside beyond the trees surrounding the campsites.

Campsites 15, 17, 19, and 22 are outside this loop and thus provide views through large and open stands of trees to the nearby lake. These sites are quite large and offer the best camping areas in the park. Wide gravel cartways provide easy access to generous areas for pitching a tent. Site 17 is the most private of these sites, while sites 16, 18, 20, and 21 are inside-loop sites but share the hardwood canopy and other site amenities. There is a trail between sites 18 and 20 that leads from the campground pathway to a trail behind the loop that follows along the upper slopes of Annie Battle Lake below.

Site 22 is large, open, and spacious with a view of the lake. Site 23 is inside the loop near the north end of the campground, while site 24 is small and off by itself but easily visible from the trail.

Sites 25 and 26 are probably the least appealing sites. Each is very near the parking lot, which is convenient but imaginably more noisy than other sites that are farther away. These are not particularly private sites, either.

Overall, this campground offers spacious sites under an impressive forest of Minnesota hardwoods. Although access is on foot, the distances are short, and the use of camp carts makes this a modest effort with pleasant rewards.

Glendalough is noted for its birding and wildlife viewing along 11 miles of hiking trails. There are more than 5 miles of surfaced bike trails (which connect to other trails that lead into the town of Battle Lake) and more than 2 miles of routes for mountain bikers. Skiers can also enjoy 8 miles of groomed trails. Late-August visitors may see migrating monarch butterflies pass through the park.

Seasonal rentals include bicycles and various watercraft, from canoes to paddleboats to stand-up paddleboards. Snowshoes and skis are available for open-country or cross-country skiers to enjoy 8 miles of groomed trails in winter.

For those wanting a camping experience that includes excellent fishing and clear-water paddling, Glendalough is a good choice. This park also features remote paddle-in campsites (which can also be accessed by backpack, bike, or sled) and two yurts, all reservable and located across the lake from the campground.

Glendalough State Park Campground

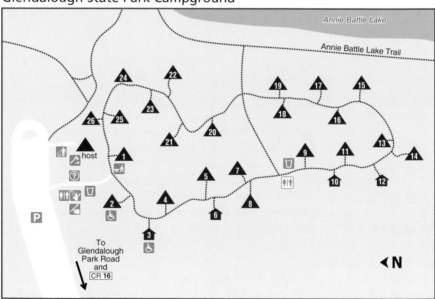

GETTING THERE

From Battle Lake go north 1.5 miles on MN 78, then east 1.8 miles on CR 16 to the park entrance on the left.

GPS COORDINATES: N46° 19.688' W95° 40.131'

30

⛺ Lake Elmo Park Reserve Campground

Beauty ★★★ / Privacy ★★★★ / Spaciousness ★★★ / Quiet ★★★★ / Security ★★★ / Cleanliness ★★★

Five ample, easily accessible, and pleasantly primitive walk-in sites are set into the woods in a park offering many activities.

I've always liked Lake Elmo Park Reserve. It's within minutes of downtown Saint Paul and yet offers wide-open spaces, rolling hills, and clusters of woodlands scattered around several lakes. It also offers a variety of modern facilities and activities with ample opportunity to take long hikes through open spaces and pitch a tent in a woodsy walk-in campsite.

There are three types of campgrounds at Lake Elmo: modern, with the tight loops and close-proximity site configuration; rustic camping, a new designation for what is also the equestrian area; and primitive, which is my favorite. Because you can park within about 150 yards of the farthest site, I decided that these five tent sites could qualify as drive-to sites. The few extra steps are worth it!

The modern sites are open, attract the RV crowd, and have little shade. However, the shrubby vegetation, made up mostly of sumac, Amur maple, and dogwood (primarily landscape accent plantings), provides a little privacy and gives a sense of personal space within the grounds' four loops.

The bucolic campsite setting in the Rustic Loop

KEY INFORMATION

ADDRESS: 1515 Keats Ave., Lake Elmo, MN 55042

CONTACT: 651-430-8370; www.co.wash ington.mn.us/502/lake-elmo-park-reserve

OPERATED BY: Washington County Parks

OPEN: Early May–mid-October

SITES: 76 electric, 5 primitive (walk-in), 20 equestrian (rustic)

EACH SITE HAS: Open tent area, picnic table, fire ring

WHEELCHAIR ACCESS: Sites 32 and 33

ASSIGNMENT: All reservable

REGISTRATION: At park office; reserve at 651-430-8370 or washingtoncounty .maxgalaxy.net/campground.aspx

FACILITIES: Restrooms, shower, water, electricity at all drive-in sites

PARKING: 1 vehicle/site; at trailhead to walk-in sites; guest parking lot; must park on gravel pad

FEES: Nonelectric: $19/night Monday–Thursday, $23/night Friday–Sunday. 20-/50-amp electric: $25–$27/night Monday–Thursday, $29–$31/night Friday–Sunday. 50-amp electric and water: $33/night Monday–Thursday, $37/night Friday–Sunday. Walk-in: $19/night Monday–Thursday, $23/night Friday–Sunday and holidays. $7 daily vehicle fee, $30 annual permit, $8 reservation fee

---

RESTRICTIONS:

PETS: Not permitted

QUIET HOURS: 10 p.m.–8 a.m.

FIRES: In fire rings or grills only; gathering firewood not permitted; firewood must be purchased from approved vendor

ALCOHOL: Not permitted

OTHER: 1 tent/site; 8 people/site; 7-day stay limit; fireworks prohibited

---

Of the modern sites, I suggest you try sites 55–59; these are at least backed by a wooded area. There are no tent sites across the road from this series, either, so you get a little more privacy. Beyond this string of acceptable sites are sites 60 and 61, which begin the fourth campground loop. These two sites also back up to the stand of trees flanking this end of the modern campground. The remaining 69 sites are open, clustered, and typical. Definitely opt for those listed above or, better yet, push for the primitive area.

The primitive hike-in camping sites are small, open, and close to the road. They border an open meadow in a bucolic setting—quite pleasant, actually. You will give up any sense of privacy at these sites, but if relaxing in a meadow amid vast fields of grass and wildflowers is what you desire, this is the spot for you. Five primitive walk-in campsites make up the string of sites in this section. Access is from the parking lot at the Nordic Center, along a 10-foot-wide grassy lane that follows the edge of the woods as spurs to each campsite intersect it at short intervals.

Site 1 is hidden by the edge of the forest that surrounds the small lake behind the first four sites. The campsite is modest: fire ring, picnic table, and tent space. Bur oak and ash are the main shade trees. A trail from camp threads through the understory and heads down to the lake. Site 2 has a small, earthen tent area; is flanked by shade trees; and has its own private walking path down to the lake. Site 3 is a short distance away—here your neighbor's volume level will dictate the peace and quiet this spot will afford. Site 3 is less shady than the other sites, providing its own view of the lake through the underbrush as well as access to it via the earthen trail.

Site 4, just beyond site 3, is situated on a flat area right above the lake's shore. This spot's earthen floor was covered with less grass than the other sites, so it might be a bit muddy after a prolonged rain. Another concern is that this site lies only about 5 yards off the grass access trail. Heavy foot traffic will be more noticeable from site 4 than from any other site in the primitive area.

The last primitive site, 5, is across from the access path to site 4. It sits back through a mature stand of aspens. It is also on a slope that rises from the lake and campsites 1–4 below, making it the only campsite in this group not near the small lake. Any of these sites would be a pleasant camping area for those who enjoy a more rustic experience. They sit halfway between Lake Elmo and Eagle Point Lake. (Much of Lake Elmo Park Reserve's 3.5 square miles of land—80% of it—is set aside for preservation and protection, and within that 80% lie two big lakes: Elmo and Eagle Point.)

Lake Elmo is a 206-acre lake with a depth of 130 feet and is the reserve's fishing hole. A boat ramp and a fishing pier are along its shore. A special swimming pond has been created on land, just inland from the natural lake. This safe and clean swimming spot is a sandy-bottomed swimming area (4 feet deep at its deepest) with a lifeguard for most of the summer.

Eagle Point Lake covers 143 acres. It is a good canoeing lake and serves as a focal point for one of the park's many hiking loops. A parking lot off the main park road puts hikers at one of several entry points on the lake's 3.7-mile loop.

The hike follows the lake's shoreline, taking you for a stroll through the meadows and along the forested areas of the western section of the reserve. This trail links with a half dozen other pathways that head even farther into the park's remote western and northwestern hill country. One loop follows the northern park boundary and connects with other trail networks at the equestrian campground. Other activities include fishing and bird-watching. Lighted and groomed trails provide opportunities for evening hiking and cross-country skiing.

Lake Elmo Park Reserve: Hike-In Campground

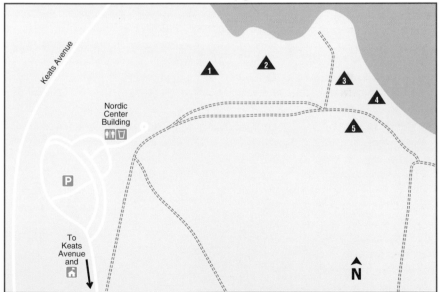

Lake Elmo Park Reserve: Rustic Loop

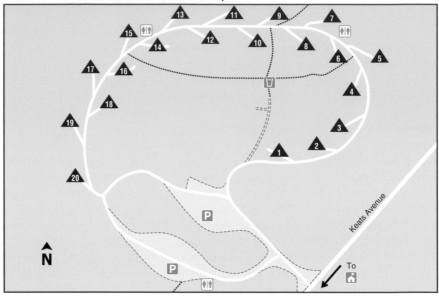

GETTING THERE

From Saint Paul head east on I-94; about 3 miles east of the intersection of I-694, turn left (north) at Exit 251 on CR 19 (Keats Avenue), and go about 1.5 miles to the park entrance.

GPS COORDINATES: N44° 58.859' W92° 53.927'

31

Maplewood State Park Campgrounds

Beauty ★★★★ / Privacy ★★★ / Spaciousness ★★★★ / Quiet ★★★★ / Security ★★★★★ / Cleanliness ★★★★

Rolling hills are dotted with lakes amid a forest of hardwoods that dazzles with fall brilliance.

Four campgrounds are spread throughout the lush northern hardwood forested hills of Maplewood State Park. Each is adjacent to one of the many lakes within the park's boundaries, providing easy road access to fishing and boating opportunities throughout this rolling-hills landscape.

Grass Lake Campground consists of five loops, three of which are adjacent to each other along the eastern shore of the lake. Another is laid out on a knoll above the southern end of the same lake, and one lies to the north set away from the lake. The main section features 32 open, moderately spaced sites. There's ample room for tents or RV rigs and not much privacy due to the openness of this particular campground.

Woodsy setting in north loop of main campground

KEY INFORMATION

ADDRESS: 39721 Park Entrance Road, Pelican Rapids, MN 56572

CONTACT: 218-863-8383, dnr.state.mn.us/state_parks/maplewood

OPERATED BY: Minnesota DNR, Division of Parks and Recreation

OPEN: Year-round (water/showers: mid-May–early October)

SITES: 71 (32 with electric), 3 backpack-in, 24 equestrian, 5 camper cabins, 1 group

EACH SITE HAS: Open tent area, picnic table, fire ring

WHEELCHAIR ACCESS: Sites 2, 13, and 19

ASSIGNMENT: Reservations required (same-day reservations available)

REGISTRATION: Reserve at 866-85-PARKS (72757) or tinyurl.com/mnspreservations

FACILITIES: Water and showers (seasonal), boat ramp, swimming beach

PARKING: 1 vehicle/site (2 vehicles/site with permission); adjacent to restrooms in main loop of Grass Lake Campground

FEES: $23/night, $17/night off-season, $31/night electric sites, $25/night electric sites off-season, $7 daily permit, $35 annual permit, $8.50 reservation fee

---

RESTRICTIONS:

PETS: On 6-foot leash; attended at all times

QUIET HOURS: 10 p.m.–8 a.m.

FIRES: In fire rings; gathering firewood not permitted; firewood must be purchased from approved vendor

ALCOHOL: Not permitted

OTHER: 6 people/site; closed to visitors 10 p.m.–8 a.m.; fireworks and metal detectors prohibited

Of the campsites in this section, sites 11–12 look particularly inviting to larger, motorized rigs, while site 15 is right along the lake, adjacent to a big space next to the fishing dock. Sites 2, 13, and 19 are the only wheelchair-accessible campsites in this park. The most shrubbery in this campground is along the pathway linking the head of each loop at lakeside with each neighboring loop.

The upper section of Grass Lake Campground is called Hollow Loop and, as the name implies, is the more wooded area, offering 13 sites in a teardrop shape. The sites are well spaced out, offering much more privacy than the main section. Sites 33 and 34 are small areas right along the road, site 34 has a pond behind it (which could mean mosquitoes), site 35 is a large site nearer to the road, and sites 36–37 are in a clearing on a gentle slope.

Site 38 is comparatively small, just the opposite of site 39, which has a large pull-in area with a couple of places to pitch tents. Site 40 has a few small (and gravelly) areas for tents. Site 41 sits back from the roadway and offers more privacy than others in this loop; therefore, it gets the nod for the choicest site in the Hollow Loop. The last few sites in this loop are small and offer little privacy.

The most rustic loop in Maplewood is situated atop a knoll overlooking Grass Lake. The Knoll Loop includes 14 tent sites and one of five camper cabins in the park. The drive into these particular sites quickly sets the mood. The road follows along a ridgeline atop rolling hills, through a cluster of sumac near the entrance to the Knoll Loop campground.

Site 46 is the first of 14 sites (plus the cabin), and although it's very exposed, it does offer a pleasant view of the lake. Site 47 sits at the end of a long driveway, its dense understory providing privacy; this is one of my preferred sites in this loop. Sites 48–52 are small, but each has a view of the lake through the trees. Site 53 is just beyond the cabin site and has a big pull-in driveway with several tent site options. It's nestled into the trees at the foot of a knoll that rises up beyond this end of the loop.

The rest of the campsites sit beyond the modest lake views and offer less privacy than others in this loop. This is a quaint loop, away by itself, nestled peacefully within the knolls that cradle the southern end of Grass Lake.

Another campground is at Lake Lida. Half of the campsites are in a loop that offers some vegetation throughout sites that tend to be best suited for smaller tents. Site 74 is a big, sloping site that sits atop an embankment that extends down to the lake. The last two sites on the west loop are open areas for small tents.

Another five campsites, all of which are open and exposed and offer little privacy, are aligned along another loop at Lake Lida. I would treat this as an overflow campsite option, while others might enjoy its lake views and road access to the nearby swimming area and boat launching sites that Lake Lida offers for all park visitors.

This is a vibrantly colorful park, with forests blanketing rolling hills and shorelines of myriad lakes. Its roads offer miles of driving-tour opportunities to view wildlife, while its lakes are popular fishing holes, drawing anglers from throughout western Minnesota. There are 25 miles of hiking trails, 10 miles (5 of which are groomed) of ski trails, and 20 miles of snowmobile trails throughout the park. In 2017 the year-round interpretive site Sugar Shack opened, with maple syrup production programs offered in the spring—an appropriate addition to a state park named Maplewood! It's among the gems in the Department of Natural Resources' jewelry chest of parks.

Lake Lida Campground and Grass Lake Campground: Main Loop

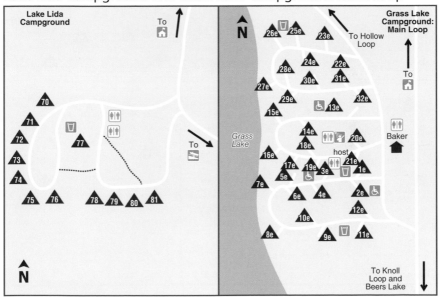

Lakes and forested hills are highlights throughout this park.

Grass Lake Campground: Knoll and Hollow Loops

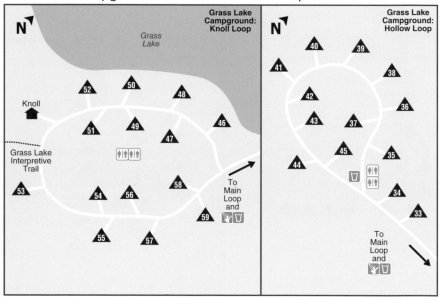

GETTING THERE

From Pelican Rapids head east on MN 108 for 7 miles to the park entrance on the right.

GPS COORDINATES: N46° 31.395' W95° 56.464'

32

Mille Lacs Kathio State Park Campgrounds

Beauty ★★★★ / Privacy ★★★ / Spaciousness ★★★ / Quiet ★★★ / Security ★★★ / Cleanliness ★★★★

This camp is rich in American Indian heritage and nestled in a hardwood forest amid rolling glacial terrain.

This area is typical of the lakes region of Minnesota, where glaciers played a major role. Besides the 18-mile-wide Mille Lacs Lake (which is the remnant of a much larger lake), the evidence of that ice age history is in the hills formed by the glacial moraine of those receding rivers of ice. Take those hills and cover them with second-generation growth of maples, oaks, and other hardwoods, and you have Mille Lacs Kathio State Park. Add a few spruce tree clusters here and there, and you've made this park one of the prettier ones in the state. The fall colors alone are a reason to visit here.

The Mille Lacs area is rich in American Indian history, from ancient tribes from the Old Copper Tradition, dating back more than 4,000 years, to the early Dakota people, a band called the Mdewakanton—"the people who live by the water of the Great Spirit." More recently, the area has been inhabited by Ojibwe, a band of northern woodland Indians who drove the Dakota farther west onto the plains.

Today the popularity of Mille Lacs Kathio is tied to the lake, famous for its walleye fishing. The lake is also the origin of the Rum River—a river much used for recreation by the time it reaches the cities just north of Minneapolis. The river flows out of Ogechie Lake, itself a small lake formed by a stream flowing out of Mille Lacs. Fishing and boating are two popular pastimes at this park.

Ogechie Campground is closest to the lake of the same name. Campsites 1–26 are in the higher elevations of the park. The sites are moderately small but are staggered

Easy canoe access to the Rum River from within the park

KEY INFORMATION

ADDRESS: 15066 Kathio State Park Road, Onamia, MN 56359

CONTACT: 320-532-3523, dnr.state.mn.us /state_parks/mille_lacs_kathio

OPERATED BY: Minnesota DNR, Division of Parks and Recreation

OPEN: Year-round (facilities: May–mid-October; water and restrooms available year-round at Trail Center)

SITES: 66 (21 with electric), 3 walk-in, 4 back-pack-in, 10 equestrian, 5 camper cabins, 1 group

EACH SITE HAS: Open tent area (some with tent pads), picnic table, fire ring

WHEELCHAIR ACCESS: Sites 44 and 45

ASSIGNMENT: Reservations required (same-day reservations available)

REGISTRATION: Reserve at 866-85-PARKS (72757) or tinyurl.com/mnspreservations

FACILITIES: Restroom, showers, water, Dumpster, RV sanitation station

PARKING: 1 vehicle/site; at trailhead parking area for walk-in sites; first loop of Petaga Campground

FEES: $23/night, $17/night off-season, $31/ night electric sites, $25/night electric sites off-season, $7 daily permit, $35 annual permit, $8.50 reservation fee

---

RESTRICTIONS:

PETS: On 6-foot leash; attended at all times

QUIET HOURS: 10 p.m.–8 a.m.

FIRES: In fire rings; gathering firewood not permitted; firewood must be purchased from approved vendor

ALCOHOL: Not permitted

OTHER: 6 people/site; closed to visitors 10 p.m.–8 a.m.; fireworks and metal detectors prohibited

---

throughout the campground to offer a bit of privacy from campers across the road. A solid alder and birch understory provides additional screening between sites. It's a better layout than most Minnesota state park campgrounds. The variety of tall oaks and maples makes the area seem more northern in setting than it really is (it's only about 80 miles from the Twin Cities).

The Petaga Campground is a multiuse cluster of drive-in campsites, walk-ins, and cabins. Sites 27–63 are long and staggered—and the first choice of the RV crowd. Sites 44 and 45 are wheelchair accessible. There is ample vegetation between the sites, and the bur oak overstory makes the long, narrow sites somewhat private. However, turnouts and the long pull-ins indicate that this is where the big-wheeled units need to camp.

Just across the park road from the lower site are the walk-ins, five cabins, and what must be considered the overflow campground. The walk-ins and the overflow are the most private and most secluded camping areas in the park.

The three walk-in sites, 64–66, are up a ridge only 30–50 yards from the parking lot at the end of the cabin road cul-de-sac. Although they share the same knoll, they are spaced well apart. A water source, parking, and a toilet are right at the base of the trail leading to the three sites.

Stuck behind the cabins are four more tent sites. These spin off from the cul-de-sac spur leading from the main park road. Each site is well apart from the others and within an easy walk of a main trail spur. With water and a toilet at the start of the camping circle, these four tent sites seem to me the best place to camp, even if they are in the distant backyard of the cabins. This separate group of campsites may look out of place on the map—and even as you drive in—but it works.

Hiking is a big activity in this park. In early spring expect to see the forest floor covered in beautiful, white blooming trilliums throughout the park. In the northern section, trails are networked around and over countless hills and valleys carved from the ancient terminal moraine. You can hike to the observation tower (on shared horse trails—be careful) or to several sites along the shore of Ogechie Lake. Trails cut close to each of the two main campgrounds. An elongated loop of horse trails cuts through the center of the park; hikers can also use this trail, although hiking is probably more enjoyable where horses aren't allowed.

A leisurely paddle by canoe or kayak is possible by putting in at a boat ramp at the end of the road that goes past the group camp. You can then paddle upstream into Ogechie Lake or take the current downriver to Shakopee Lake, where a boat landing on the southern shore is right on County Road 26 (it's about 2.5 miles back to the park entrance).

Wildlife viewers will have many opportunities to witness hawks, ospreys, owls, and eagles in action. A bird list is available at the park office. Deer, beavers, and raccoons are also common within the park. Other park activities and amenities include a picnic and playground area, a swimming beach, an interpretive center, boat rental, fishing, and riding trails. Outside the park and just a few miles north on US 169 is an American Indian museum that showcases the proud heritage of the people of this area. Whether it's cultural or geological history or the richly colored and lush hardwood forest setting, Mille Lacs Kathio offers a better-than-average camping experience for those who decide to pitch their tent here.

Mille Lacs Kathio State Park Campgrounds

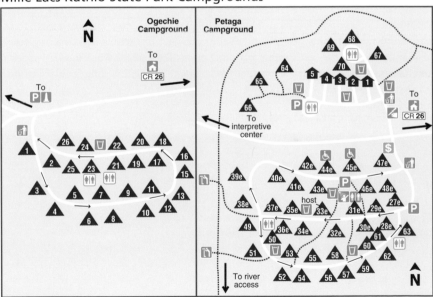

GETTING THERE

From Onamia go 7 miles north on US 169 to CR 26. Turn left (south) on CR 26 and go 0.7 mile to the park entrance on the right.

GPS COORDINATES: N46° 7.691' W93° 46.063'

33

Monson Lake State Park Campground

Beauty ★★★ / Privacy ★★★ / Spaciousness ★★★ / Quiet ★★★ / Security ★★★ / Cleanliness ★★★★

A peaceful lakeside setting is nestled into the rolling fields and farm landscape on the edge of the Minnesota west-central prairie.

Crossing this park's northern boundary sets the mood for this laid-back island of shady oak, maple, and ash. The road winds down a gravel lane as it draws you toward this small park situated between two lakes in the middle of rolling prairie hills.

Glacial action, a product of the Wadena lobe approximately 30,000 years ago, formed the gentle hills and expanses of sand, gravel, and boulders. It also left big chunks of ice pressed into the ground as the massive sheets of ice receded. When that ice thawed out, it left water-filled impressions in this piece of prairie in western Minnesota. Monson Lake and neighboring West Sunburg Lake were thus formed—all to the eventual delight of anglers and canoeists who now come to enjoy camping at the modest campground nestled between these two lakes.

Historically speaking, Monson Lake was the site of one of the earliest battles in Minnesota's Dakota Conflict. Swedish settlers clashed with a local band of Dakota, making it one of the first skirmishes in that war. In 1926 local residents purchased a few acres to memorialize the settlers, the Broberg and Lundborg families, and in 1938 the land became a state park. Over the years more land was added to the park, which now encompasses 346 acres.

It's pretty much a fishing lake, but there is ample shoreline with small bays to give everyone a chance to enjoy the water either paddling or casting a line toward shore. Besides great fishing for lunker bass, the park has excellent bird-watching, including regular sightings of

Monson Lake from the boat launch area next to the campgrounds

KEY INFORMATION

ADDRESS: 1690 15th St. NE, Sunburg, MN 56289

CONTACT: 320-354-2055, dnr.state.mn.us /state_parks/monson_lake

OPERATED BY: Minnesota DNR, Division of Parks and Recreation (managed by Sibley State Park)

OPEN: Early May–October (facilities: late May–mid-September)

SITES: 20 campsites (6 electric)

EACH SITE HAS: Open tent area, picnic table, fire ring

WHEELCHAIR ACCESS: No designated sites

ASSIGNMENT: All reservable

REGISTRATION: Reserve at 866-85-PARKS (72757) or tinyurl.com/mnspreservations

FACILITIES: Vault toilet, water, picnic pavilion, boat ramp; seasonal flush toilets and showers

PARKING: 1 vehicle/site; by boat ramp and picnic pavilion

FEES: $19/night, $15/night off-season, $27/ night electric sites, $23/night electric sites off-season, $7 daily permit, $35 annual permit, $8.50 reservation fee

---

RESTRICTIONS:

PETS: On 6-foot leash; attended at all times

QUIET HOURS: 10 p.m.–8 a.m.

FIRES: In fire rings; gathering firewood not permitted; firewood must be purchased from approved vendor

ALCOHOL: Not permitted

OTHER: 6 people/site; closed to visitors 10 p.m.–8 a.m.; fireworks and metal detectors prohibited

---

white pelicans, a variety of heron, western grebes, and other waterfowl. Canoeists on Monson Lake can access neighboring West Sunburg Lake to the east via a 150-yard portage at the northeast section of Monson Lake. A 1-mile hiking trail winds through stands of oak, ash, and basswood, the main tree species of the area.

The campground loop begins just before the boat ramp. Half of the campsites are within thick stands of hardwood trees along the lake's edge. Site 1 is wide open, set back deep into the trees. Site 2 looks down over the ramp and out onto the lake. It's a gorgeous site, typical of those along the top of the slope leading down to the water. Most of the lakeside sites are exposed to the road, but the trees help maintain a qualified cozy setting. Site 1 is a small, exposed site. Site 3 sits amid a lush array of towering, shade-producing hardwoods. Even-numbered sites 4–12 are all on the lake side of the loop. Site 6 is fairly exposed compared to others, while site 5 is big enough for an RV unit. Site 7 offers a bit more privacy than others, due to a natural screen that grows between the tent site and the roadway.

Site 8 is my choice for the best tent site at Monson Lake. It just has that look about it—surrounded by the same trees, overlooking the same lake—yet it's especially appealing as a roomy, woodsy campsite. Site 9 is rather small, very close to the road, but still appealing due to a tight cluster of trees and view of the lake. Site 10 offers an especially pleasant view of the lake. The last three sites along the lake, 11–13, are the least private of this stretch. Sites 11 and 12 are small, open sites totally visible from the road. Site 13 is right next to a walking trail, and its driveway is the full width of the campsite. No privacy here, either, but another good view of the lake. Despite the openness, these sites are still cozy places to pitch your tent.

The remaining campsites are on the back side of the campground loop and therefore out of view of the lake. They are adjacent to the picnic area and are the most exposed in the park. Site 14 is right off the road, with an unobscured view out toward the open, grassy lawn of the picnic area. Sites 15 and 17 are laid out on an open lawn area with very few trees between the sites. Site 16 is within a cluster of trees but remains a very exposed site. Site 18 is also in the woods and is also open and spacious. It does, however, have an inviting appeal that makes it my choice of sites on this side of the loop that does not face the lake. Site 20 is an open site that would serve well as a larger, multitent site.

Monson Lake is roughly the same distance from Benson as it is from Spicer. Benson offers a water park, a golf course, and access to the Chippewa River, one of western Minnesota's prime canoeing rivers. The New London–Spicer area is known for having wonderful lakes for swimming, fishing, and boating. However, the bucolic setting of Monson Lake, the excellent fishing and birding, and a day's worth of canoeing opportunities make this campground worth a stay for its own sake.

Monson Lake State Park Campground

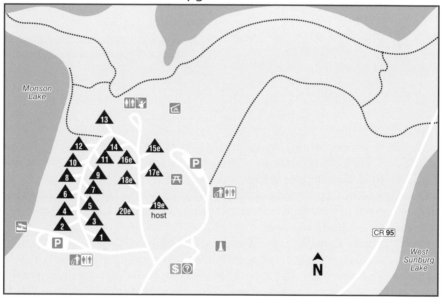

GETTING THERE

From Benson go 16 miles east on MN 9 or west 2 miles from Sunburg. Turn south on CR 95 and go about 2.5 miles to the park entrance on the right. From Willmar go north on CR 5 for 15 miles to MN 9. Turn west (left) and go about 9.5 miles to CR 95. Turn right on CR 95; the park entrance will be on your left.

GPS COORDINATES: N45° 19.172' W95° 16.535'

34

⚠ Sibley State Park Campgrounds

Beauty ★★★ / Privacy ★★★ / Spaciousness ★★★ / Quiet ★★★ / Security ★★★ / Cleanliness ★★★★

Serpentine, tree-covered ridges and hills in an old forest setting characterize Sibley.

Seems like every state park in southern Minnesota is located at the heart or edge of a key natural history area. This is no truer than at Sibley State Park, situated in that area of Minnesota where the eastern edge of the expansive great prairies meets the hardwood forests of the Big Woods region beyond those grasses. It's an area where an even more ancient history reveals a landscape strewn with the rock and rubble from four glaciated periods.

The lake and hills of Sibley Park are geological reminders of the receding ice fields and melting monolithic chunks of glaciers that left their mark on this region of not only Minnesota but also the entire upper Midwest. The shoreline of the lake drops away sharply to the bottom—no long, sloping shelf. These are glacier-born lakes—bodies of water formed when glacial ice, once embedded in the landscape, melted. Those lakes are surrounded by ridges and hills formed when gigantic drain fields from retreating ice melts spewed gravel and boulders out across the plains. Today, those harsh reminders are subdued by tree-lined hills, ridges, and knolls and by flowing prairie grasses with clusters of renegade sumacs and the occasional gnarly oak sapling.

That topography in miniature describes Oak Ridge, the upper campground at Sibley. The site is forested with mature oaks, maple, and ash—all classic big-tree species. This

The observation decks atop Mount Tom with sweeping vistas of the park and beyond

KEY INFORMATION

ADDRESS: 800 Sibley Park Road NE, New London, MN 56273

CONTACT: 320-354-2055, dnr.state.mn.us /state_parks/sibley

OPERATED BY: Minnesota DNR, Division of Parks and Recreation

OPEN: Mid-April–November (facilities: early May–mid-October)

SITES: 129 (87 with electric), 9 equestrian, 5 camper cabins, 3 walk-in group

EACH SITE HAS: Open tent area (some with tent pads), picnic table, fire ring

WHEELCHAIR ACCESS: Sites 40, 41, 71, 73, 75, 98, 106, and 129

ASSIGNMENT: All reservable

REGISTRATION: Reserve at 866-85-PARKS (72757) or tinyurl.com/mnspreservations

FACILITIES: Restrooms, showers, water, trailer dump station

PARKING: 1 vehicle/site; on right just before entering Lakeview Campground

FEES: $23/night, $17/night off-season, $31/ night electric sites, $25/night electric sites off-season, $7 daily permit, $35 annual permit, $8.50 reservation fee

RESTRICTIONS:

PETS: On 6-foot leash; attended at all times

QUIET HOURS: 10 p.m.–8 a.m.

FIRES: In fire rings; gathering firewood not permitted; firewood must be purchased from approved vendor

ALCOHOL: Not permitted

OTHER: 6 people/site; closed to visitors 10 p.m.–8 a.m.; fireworks and metal detectors prohibited

defined overstory has an equally mature and dense understory. The first irregularly shaped loop, containing campsites 75–98, straddles a line of open savanna–like grasses and an oak scrub that quickly develops into a thick canopy within a few campsites of the entrance to this loop. Each site is tucked back into the surrounding vegetation with the standard fire ring and picnic table. Site 75 is wheelchair accessible.

The staggered entrance driveway to each site along a narrow, serpentine road creates secluded and private camping sites throughout the first loop. As the road winds back out from the campgrounds, the last few sites, 92–95, become more open again. Site 98 is wheelchair accessible.

The second loop contains sites 99–131, which are all laid out in an open array with little understory. The middle section of this hilly campground becomes more wooded as you approach sites 106–121. Sites 106 and 129 are wheelchair accessible.

Toilet stations and a restroom and shower unit, along with the six water pumps scattered throughout the two loops, give all campers easy access.

The lower campground, Lakeview, offers extra-spacious sites on the standard gridlike layout seen at many state parks. Box elders and maples dominate the forested area that is otherwise so open it resembles a picnic area—and an RV park. That said, campsites 66–68 and 70 at least merge into the uncluttered woods behind each of those sites, offering a bit of the better life of tent camping. Sites 40, 41, 71, and 73 are wheelchair accessible.

No matter which loop or site you choose, take some time to check out the hiking trails— all 18 miles' worth. Make sure you include the trail that leads up to the all-encompassing vantage point at the top of Mount Tom. There you'll enjoy a colorful panoramic vista of the forests and countryside. The passage along the paved trail that winds through a quaint stand of oaks as it climbs to the summit soon reveals the 360-degree view. Your imagination may help you create a prehistoric landscape of mile-high ice fields covering this area. A trip to the summit of Mount Tom at the height of fall color would be one well worth planning. Other activities include naturalist programs, horseback riding, biking, hiking, swimming, fishing, and boating. Canoe, kayak, boat, and snowshoe rentals are available seasonally at the Beach Store.

Pay close attention when hiking the network of trails; they may reveal some of the park's critters—white-tailed deer, ruffed grouse, foxes, and more. The marsh areas are great for wildlife viewing; watch for puddle ducks, egrets, and a variety of songbirds.

The rumpled hills, winding roads, and mature stands all create a deep-woods setting laced with hiking trails and dotted with lakes—a camper's delight.

Sibley State Park Campgrounds

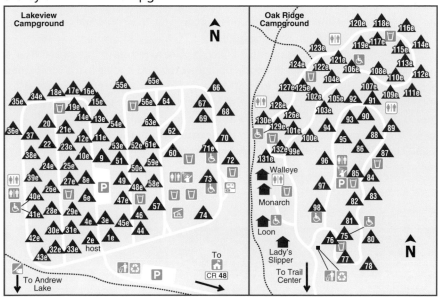

GETTING THERE

From Willmar go 15 miles north on US 71 to CR 48. Take a left onto CR 48 and go about 1 mile to the park entrance.

GPS COORDINATES: N45° 18.815' W95° 1.964'

35

⛺ Snake River Campground

Beauty ★★★ / Privacy ★★★ / Spaciousness ★★★ / Quiet ★★★★ / Security ★★★ / Cleanliness ★★★★

Bring your canoe to this charming setting with the Snake River as a backdrop.

Any campground tucked among the towering mixed pines along a medium-size canoeing river is a good choice in my book. So it is with the Snake River State Forest campground just east of Pine City. This is within Minnesota's Chengwatana State Forest, a glacier-sculpted country of hills covered in a modest mix of white and red pines with an occasional jack pine and clumps of paper birch. It's also a terrain of marshes and three notable rivers: the Kettle, Snake, and St. Croix. Although the Snake doesn't carry the lofty Wild and Scenic River status of its companions, it's a fun river to paddle.

For hikers, the Snake River Campground offers a place to rest, as well as access to the Matthew Lourey State Trail. This multiuse trail cuts across the road leading to the campground—right inside the entrance after you turn off County Road 8. Paddlers are attracted to this campground, as the Snake River is also one of Minnesota's official State Water Trails.

You know you are getting closer to the north country when you see notices about black bears on the information bulletin board. The warning is not exclusive to the Snake River sites and should be heeded as a general practice; common sense should prevail when preparing or storing food.

Campsite tucked back into the edge of the woods

KEY INFORMATION

ADDRESS: Snake River Campground Road, 0.5 mile north of St. Croix Road, Pine City, MN 55063

CONTACT: Wild River State Park: 651-583-2125; Minnesota DNR, Division of Forestry, 651-296-6157, dnr.state.mn.us/state_forests/facilities/cmp00008

OPERATED BY: Chengwatana State Forest (managed by Wild River State Park)

OPEN: April–November

SITES: 26 rustic

EACH SITE HAS: Open tent area, picnic table, fire ring

WHEELCHAIR ACCESS: Sites 20 and 21

ASSIGNMENT: First come, first served

REGISTRATION: Fee station inside first loop

FACILITIES: Vault toilets, water

PARKING: 1 vehicle/site; on left before first loop

FEES: $14/night

RESTRICTIONS:

PETS: On 6-foot leash; attended at all times

QUIET HOURS: 10 p.m.–8 a.m.

FIRES: In fire rings; gathering downed or dead firewood permitted; firewood must be purchased from approved vendor

ALCOHOL: Not permitted

OTHER: 8 people/site; closed to visitors 10 p.m.–8 a.m.; fireworks and metal detectors prohibited

Campsites are laid out along two loops under a canopy of white and red pines and other mixed near-north species. These sites usually sit back off the roadway and have ample understory for privacy and security. Each site is laid out with the standard-issue picnic table and fire ring. There are no designated pads for a tent, just plenty of grassy spaces on which to pitch it.

Sites 1–5 are spaced far apart on either side of the first loop, situated under a canopy of red pines. Site 5 sits up from the river by itself with only the picnic area nearby. There is only one picnic table in this area, but it's a great place to get close to the river without going through a campsite.

Site 6 backs up to another site (16) in the next loop but is really the only campsite so situated—yet even it is spacious. The rest of the sites in this first loop are spread out, staggered off the main loop, and spacious. Site 11 is close to the main road, making it the least desirable site in this loop.

The second loop offers more sites backing up to the river. Site 12 is more open than most of the sites in this campground, but like the rest it is in a staggered layout, so there's privacy and room to play as well. Sites 14 and 15 are in a cluster of white and red pine. Sites 16 (close to 6 in the first loop) and 17 are nondescript, but they are private and spacious.

Sites 18 and 19 are at the head of the loop and up from the big 90-degree bend that the Snake River takes at this point in the campground. These sites located up from the river usually have a well-worn path leading from the campsite to the bank. In fact, there is a defined trail between sites 18 and 19 that leads down to the river from the loop. It connects to an informal but defined trail that heads up- and downstream from that point.

Sites 20 and 22 are in the open, site 20 a little too close to the outhouse for my liking (sites 20 and 21 are wheelchair accessible). Sites 23–25 are in a stand of pines and aspen and sit on a plateau about 15 feet above the river. The river is a smooth-flowing body of water at this point, so there are no riffles or rock gardens to create any noticeable river sounds. Still, its proximity to the center of the campground makes these sites especially appealing. Site 26 is right off the road and is the smallest of the sites.

Every site at the Snake River Campground offers pleasant surroundings. The canopy of mixed pines, the spaciousness of the sites, and the river defining the boundaries on two sides all combine to create a pleasant and casual camping environment. Canoeing campers may want to consider a shuttle to enable them to either put in or take out at this campground during a weekend paddling outing. The big activities here are canoeing and fishing.

Snake River Campground

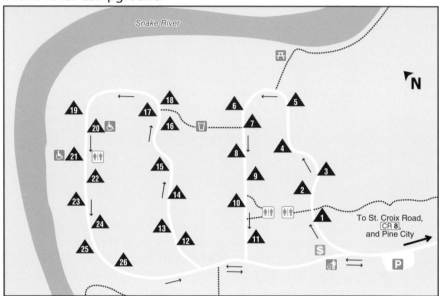

GETTING THERE

From Pine City take CR 8 (St. Croix Road) east 9.4 miles to the park entrance (Campground Road) on the left. Continue 0.5 mile north to the campground.

GPS COORDINATES: N45° 49.298' W92° 46.823'

36

Wild River State Park Campground

Beauty ★★★ / Privacy ★★★★ / Spaciousness ★★★★ / Quiet ★★★★★ / Security ★★★ / Cleanliness ★★★★

This beautifully forested park stretches several miles along the scenic and alluring St. Croix River.

Anytime you get a chance to enjoy camping along the St. Croix, do it. The farther north you can get, away from the larger communities closer to the Twin Cities, the purer the experience will be. Wild River State Park offers spacious sites, wonderful hiking trails, river access with a few shoreside campsites, and dense Minnesota hardwood forests. The park is long and narrow, stretching for a dozen or so miles right along the west bank of the Wild and Scenic St. Croix River.

Although there are several good sites within the developed campground, I've pitched my tent only at one of the backpack-in/canoe-in sites along the river. A few are close enough that you can park nearby and make short trips to the campsite. Others are a bit farther apart and are actually better accessed by the river. These are rustic sites by definition but offer a basic tent space, picnic table, fire ring, and pit toilet. The sites are in isolated spots along the river and are accessible by canoe or by the trail that follows the riverbank. If you are a self-sufficient camper who wants to be away from even the smallest gathering of tents, these

The Wild and Scenic St. Croix River, the eastern boundary of Wild River State Park

KEY INFORMATION

ADDRESS: 39797 Park Trail, Center City, MN 55012

CONTACT: 651-583-2125, dnr.state.mn.us /state_parks/wild_river

OPERATED BY: Minnesota DNR, Division of Parks and Recreation

OPEN: Year-round (water/showers: late April–late October)

SITES: 94 (34 with electric), 4 canoe-in, 7 backpack-in, 20 equestrian, 6 camper cabins, 1 guesthouse, 9 walk-in group

EACH SITE HAS: Open tent area, picnic table, fire ring

WHEELCHAIR ACCESS: Site 60

ASSIGNMENT: Reservations required (same-day reservations available)

REGISTRATION: Reserve at 866-85-PARKS (72757) or tinyurl.com/mnspreservations

FACILITIES: Restrooms and showers (not available for dispersed campers), water, RV sanitation station, boat ramps, picnic shelter, visitor center, amphitheater, trail center

PARKING: 2 vehicles/site; at head of loop D, at all boat ramps, at picnic area before campground, at trailhead to group sites, and at trailhead for backpack-in sites

FEES: $23/night, $15/night off-season, $31/ night electric sites, $23/night electric sites off-season, $7/night backpack-in, $7 daily permit, $35 annual permit, $8.50 reservation fee

---

RESTRICTIONS:

PETS: On 6-foot leash; attended at all times

QUIET HOURS: 10 p.m.–8 a.m.

FIRES: In fire rings; gathering firewood not permitted; firewood must be purchased from approved vendor

ALCOHOL: Not permitted

OTHER: 6 people/site; closed to visitors 10 p.m.–8 a.m.; fireworks and metal detectors prohibited

---

sites are for you. However, if you are bound to the land or don't want the long haul, check out the five loops at the northern end of the southern section of this park.

Oak, ash, maple, and aspen form a dense, lush forest with a solid understory in which five loops of the campground are situated. Immediately on entering loop A, you notice the spaciousness of each site. The sites are spread out, the driveways are staggered in most cases, and each site is surrounded by a thick understory providing a lot of privacy. As is the nature of a looped campground, those sites situated along the outside of the loop offer more room and less likelihood of neighbors pitching a tent too close.

Loops B and C are more open than loop A, but each loop is separated from the other to provide some room to spread out. A little creative tent pitching through these sites will ensure a seemingly private experience in the woods with few views of the tent next door or across the road.

A thick canopy of bur and red oak protects the sites in loop D (site 60 is wheelchair accessible). This is coupled with a thick understory that continues throughout loop E. As with the earlier loops, these sites are equally spacious and offer considerable privacy. At the head of each loop is a trail that directs campers to the St. Croix River flowing past the densely wooded bank just beyond the campground.

It's no surprise that the campsites are spacious—this is one of the largest parks in the state. Nearly 5,000 of its 6,800-plus acres were donated as park property by Northern States Power Company. Its human history traces back past the white pine timber days, before early fur-trading routes, and beyond even the Dakota and Ojibwe tribes to nomadic inhabitants who first settled this area more than 6,000 years ago.

The most impressive amenities of this park, besides the river and woods, are the 15 miles of hiking trails. Trails vary from the wide berth of the old military roadway running up through the center of the park to the narrow, earthen path along the river. There's even 2.5 miles of wheelchair-accessible trail. A horseback riding stable is located right outside the park to accommodate the cowpoke spirit in campers. The park provides more than 20 miles of horse trails too.

Not all of the park is wooded. The Amador Prairie is a small bluestem prairie system that seems to flow throughout the park between the islands of trees like a great sea of grass. Because of these two distinct ecosystems, and the proximity of the river and patches of marsh areas in the park, wildlife abounds. White-tailed deer find the forest/grass mix a perfect habitat, while the waterways are home or stopover spots for a variety of ducks, herons, and bitterns. Raptors such as harriers and bald eagles hunt the valleys and prairies for prey. Park activities and amenities include horseback-riding trails, biking, hiking, fishing, boat ramps, and paddling (canoe rentals available).

For wide, roomy, deep-forest camping or a weekend jaunt in the canoe with the chance at a secluded site along a Wild and Scenic River, camping at Wild River State Park ranks up there with the best of the best in my book.

Wild River State Park Campground

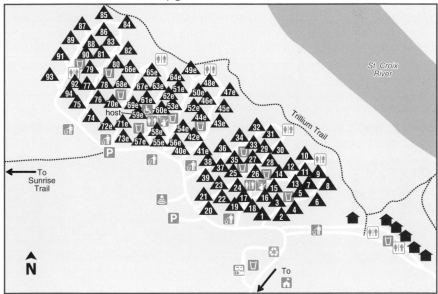

GETTING THERE

From the Twin Cities take I-35 North, and exit at MN 95 (Exit 147). Take MN 95 northeast 11 miles to Almelund. Go north on CR 12 about 3 miles to the park's main (southern) entrance.

GPS COORDINATES: N45° 32.537' W92° 44.309'

37

William O'Brien State Park Campgrounds

Beauty ★★★ / Privacy ★★★ / Spaciousness ★★★ / Quiet ★★★ / Security ★★★ / Cleanliness ★★★

This is almost like two different parks—the upper park with its forests, meadows, and hills, and the lower park with the forested, scenic St. Croix River.

I used to canoe down the St. Croix River to William O'Brien State Park from Taylor's Falls when I was in college. During all those stopovers I never once realized that there was another whole section of the park across the highway from the river. It wasn't until I explored the hiking trails in this upper section that I learned of its character and charm. Fortunately for campers seeking a more peaceful and private camping experience, both sections of the park have a few sites that make the list here.

The park features both an upper and a lower campground, each with about 60 sites. At first glance the campgrounds are characteristically "state park" in appearance. They have the standard-issue picnic table, fire ring, and drive-in parking space. The upper campground (Savanna) is made up of four loops, each to the left off the main road. This road skirts a marshy area on the west (right) side of the road. It's not until you get to the third and fourth loops, campsites 98–125, that sites are laid out along both sides of the upper campground road. This opens up possibilities—camping on the outside of the loops is usually the best option because the back of one lane of campsites doesn't back up to those in the next lane.

The trail along the banks of the St. Croix River near the lower campground

KEY INFORMATION

ADDRESS: 19074 St. Croix Trail N, Marine on St. Croix, MN 55047

CONTACT: 651-433-0500, dnr.state.mn.us /state_parks/william_obrien

OPERATED BY: Minnesota DNR, Division of Parks and Recreation

OPEN: Year-round (Savanna Campground facilities and Riverway Campground: mid-April–mid-October)

SITES: 114 (73 with electric), 2 walk-in, 4 camper cabins, 3 walk-in group, 1 group

EACH SITE HAS: Open tent area, picnic table, fire ring

WHEELCHAIR ACCESS: Sites 21, 85, and 86

ASSIGNMENT: Reservations required (same-day reservations available)

REGISTRATION: Reserve at 866-85-PARKS (72757) or tinyurl.com/mnspreservations

FACILITIES: Restrooms, showers, vault toilets, water, RV sanitation station

PARKING: 2 vehicles/site; in Savanna and Riverway Campgrounds; parking area at trailhead for walk-in sites

FEES: $23/night, $17/night off-season, $31/ night electric sites, $25/night electric sites off-season, $7 daily permit, $35 annual permit, $8.50 reservation fee

---

RESTRICTIONS:

PETS: On 6-foot leash; attended at all times

QUIET HOURS: 10 p.m.–8 a.m.

FIRES: In fire rings; gathering firewood not permitted; firewood must be purchased from approved vendor

ALCOHOL: Not permitted

OTHER: 2 tents/site; 6 people/site; closed to visitors 10 p.m.–8 a.m.; fireworks and metal detectors prohibited

The last loop is a cul-de-sac and offers about a dozen campsites, and although they are fairly open, not so private, and close to the road, they are still the preferred picks in this section.

The trails in the western half of the park (this upper section) wind through hills and meadows, around small lakes, and even across or under railroad tracks, creating a meandering country footpath network that can keep hikers trekking merrily along for miles.

Riverway is the lower cluster of sites laid out in three sections: a single loop and a loop intersected by a narrow road, creating a double loop. The odd-numbered sites 1–13 and 47–59 (and 60) are outside-loop locations that back up to trees and understory and are set back from the river.

The most alluring thing about the lower campground is the broad, promenade-like walk along the river under a canopy of red pines. Beautiful vistas of the St. Croix and the lush, hilly country across the river provide several places to stop and enjoy this splendid view as you watch canoes and boats drift past. It's clearly one of the more attractive features of any state park in the system.

The area's topography is glacial valleys and hills created from the sandstone deposited by an inland sea millions of years ago. Early settlers included the Dakota and Ojibwe. Later, the fur trade flourished, followed by a prosperous timber industry. Numerous sawmills rose up along the St. Croix until the white pines were depleted. Today the area is a rich center of tourism with Taylors Falls to the north and the bustling river town of Stillwater to the south.

Of course, William O'Brien State Park is considered a canoeist's park because of its location on the St. Croix River. Besides the attraction of paddling the river's main channel and back sloughs above and below the park, William O'Brien tends to be as popular as the take-out spot for casual river runners starting up at Interstate Park as for those putting in at the park and paddling south a dozen or so miles to Stillwater. Either way, the canoeing in this region is hot all summer long. Canoe and kayak rentals at the park office, and shuttle services and canoe rentals near the park, provide helpful services too.

So close to the Twin Cities, William O'Brien's two campgrounds offer myriad opportunities to enjoy nature, both physically and mentally. The lower camping area has the personality of a water's-edge park, and the upper park reveals the personality of its varied terrain and mixture of woods, meadows, flats, and rolling hills. It's a dual-personality park to be enjoyed fully on both fronts.

Whether you're in need of a weekend getaway or just passing through, spending some time in both halves of William O'Brien State Park will offer rewards the entire family can enjoy.

William O'Brien State Park Campgrounds

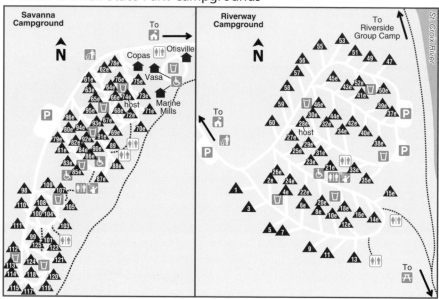

GETTING THERE

From Stillwater take MN 95 north 13 miles to the park's entrance.

GPS COORDINATES: N45° 13.523' W92° 45.814'

SOUTHERN MINNESOTA

The Mississippi River vista from an overlook near the campground in Great River Bluffs State Park (see page 137)

38

Beaver Creek Valley State Park Campgrounds

Beauty ★★★ / Privacy ★★ / Spaciousness ★★ / Quiet ★★★ / Security ★★★ / Cleanliness ★★★★

Bubbling springs are among this nature lovers' gem nestled into the valleys of southeast Minnesota's beautiful Driftless Area.

This quaint, narrow creek valley showcases the diverse flora, fauna, and geological offerings of the extreme southeastern portion of Minnesota. It offers a unique contradiction to the glacier-worn terrain common to most Midwestern states around the Great Lakes region.

Beaver Creek Valley lies in what's called the Driftless Area of glaciation. In geological terms that means this area was not covered in the last series of ice ages; therefore, there are no glacial deposits or drifts. Melted waters raging through these areas sculpted extremely deep and long valleys. Still, its makeup was directly affected by surrounding ice—massive sheets that retreated, spewing torrents of water that formed valley-gouging rivers throughout this area. Etching its way through layers of sandstone and dolomite, these unrelenting rivers carved out myriad valleys, such as those that form Beaver Creek Valley. Subsequent forestation by lowland willows, cottonwoods, and elms, and groves of maples and oaks higher up the slopes, have turned this area into a living museum of rare plants, abundant wildlife, and beautiful valleys laced with scores of spring-fed creeks. Evidence of activity by American Indians and homesteading settlers who relied on the park's resources can be found here as well.

Campsites abut Beaver Creek.

KEY INFORMATION

ADDRESS: 15954 CR 1, Caledonia, MN 55921

CONTACT: 507-724-2107; dnr.state.mn.us /state_parks/beaver_creek_valley

OPERATED BY: Minnesota DNR, Division of Parks and Recreation

OPEN: April–mid-November (facilities: May–mid-October)

SITES: 26 drive-in (16 with electric), 16 walk-in, 6 cart-in, 1 camper cabin, 1 group

EACH SITE HAS: Open tent area (2 with tent pads), picnic table, fire ring

WHEELCHAIR ACCESS: Site 15

ASSIGNMENT: All reservable

REGISTRATION: Reserve at 866-85-PARKS (72757) or tinyurl.com/mnspreservations

FACILITIES: Restrooms, showers, vault toilets, water

PARKING: At campsites, visitor center, and north entrance to Beaver Creek Valley Trail; 1 vehicle/site (2 vehicles/site with permission)

FEES: $19 ($27 electric), $15 off-season ($23 off-season electric); plus $7 daily permit, $35 annual permit, $8.50 reservation fee

---

RESTRICTIONS:

PETS: On 6-foot leash; attended at all times

QUIET HOURS: 10 p.m.–8 a.m.

FIRES: In fire rings; gathering firewood not permitted; firewood must be purchased from approved vendor

ALCOHOL: Not permitted

OTHER: 6 people/site; closed to visitors 10 p.m.–8 a.m.; fireworks and metal detectors prohibited

The most striking impressions of the park are its landscape features—each remarkable in its own visual way. Upon entering the park, campers will immediately notice the steep-walled valleys, as long, narrow, winding roads (not really conducive to battleship-size RVs) lead campers through groves of bottomland trees and into upland hardwoods to three camping areas. The road twists through the modern day-use and picnic area before reaching the first, large campground stretched out along the roadway. Its sites are more open and spacious and offer the least privacy of the three campgrounds in the park. Be advised that early spring flooding could spread to this campground (particularly sites 1–14) during spring thaw and high overflow. These are the sites most likely to be used by the RV crowd. Site 15 is designated as wheelchair accessible.

The designated tent campground is 0.25 mile farther and is nestled into the valley just beyond Big Spring, the official source of East Beaver Creek. Typical of all state parks, the sites include a pull-in driveway, picnic table, and fire ring. A pit toilet as well as restrooms and shower units are within easy walking distance.

My choice for camping here is any one of the six walk-in/group sites or six cart-in sites. Though the park offers many amenities and any site is adequate and worthwhile, the walk-in sites offer that feeling of remoteness and rusticity that reminds me of what camping has always been about—a chance to experience the outdoors, a reprieve from the madding crowd. These sites are off a cul-de-sac about 0.5 mile past the tent campground. As in most state parks, the few extra yards of carrying gear to your walk-in site are rewarded with privacy, solitude, and a sense of truly being away from it all.

If you're the inquisitive type and love nature, Beaver Creek Valley will keep you entertained and informed on many short visits or a long, active weekend. Trails follow the main flowages and take hikers up to the ridges and plateaus 250 feet above the valley floor. Beaver Valley Trail is a 5-mile out-and-back trek along the valley floor. Plateau Rock Trail rises to a ridgetop plateau on one side of the valley, and the Switchback Trail zigzags up the other side. Both reward hikers with panoramic overlooks across the valley and beyond.

One of the things I remember about this camping area is that warnings are posted around the park about the timber rattlesnake, common to this part of Minnesota but very elusive. You'd be most likely to encounter one sunning on a rock during the heat of the day. Be watchful, and if you come upon a snake, give it a wide berth, or simply backstep out of the immediate area. Caution should be taken when hiking or climbing remote trails. More likely you'll encounter the deer, foxes, raccoons, and occasional turkey that live in the park.

Beaver Creek Valley affords anglers young and old an opportunity to wet a line—the creeks are teeming with native (not stocked) brown trout. Even though Minnesota residents don't need a fishing license to fish in Minnesota state park waters (inland, not border lakes), you will need a trout stamp if you plan to fish in the waters of Beaver Creek State Park.

Catching an elusive brownie, hiking along and up steep valley trails, scouting for wildlife, or just enjoying the plethora of wildflowers that bloom throughout the summer makes Beaver Creek Valley a top choice among these already special places to camp in Minnesota.

Beaver Creek Valley State Park Campgrounds

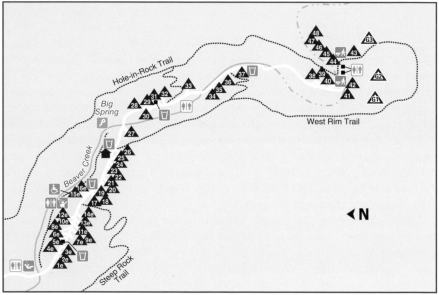

GETTING THERE

From Caledonia, take MN 76 about 1 mile north, then stay straight (west) on CR 1 for 2.5 miles to the park entrance.

GPS COORDINATES: N43° 38.474' W91° 34.828'

39

Blue Mounds State Park Campgrounds

Beauty ★★★ / Privacy ★★ / Spaciousness ★★★ / Quiet ★★★ / Security ★★★ / Cleanliness ★★★

Campers share the prairie with cacti, coyotes, and a wild herd of bison at Blue Mounds.

To geologists, the Blue Mounds are outcrops of Sioux quartzite that jut out across 1.5 miles of prairie (Blue Mounds State Park is one of the largest expanses of prairie found in the state's park system). To pioneers crossing this prairie, these bumps on the western skyline appeared blue—hence the name. Since the first three American bison were introduced here in 1961, Blue Mounds has become home to more than 60 of the animals. And for campers seeking a unique setting amid the prairies of southwestern Minnesota, Blue Mounds is an inviting natural "speed bump" that rewards those who take the time to slow down and look around.

The campgrounds are situated along Mound Creek at the northern end of the Blue Mounds outcrop. The main campground consists of 71 campsites, laid out straight down one side of the road and in three main loops on the other. The sites on the outside of each loop are more spacious, and those at the head of the first two loops also face the creek.

While most of the sites are fairly roomy, the inner campsites are open and therefore might be less appealing. This is also where the RVs and larger camping units tend to park. Each site has the standard state park amenities of a driveway, picnic table, and fire ring with a grate.

The campsites at the head of the loops are very exposed to the rest of the camp and roadway. However, by facing back toward the creek you can at least visually block out others. That's because these loops end at the edge of a small, rocky ridge a few yards above the creek. Simply step back beyond the end of the campsite, and you emerge first beneath an oak canopy, then onto a rocky ledge above the water. If this setting sounds appealing, ask

The Quarry Trail alongside a rocky ridge

KEY INFORMATION

ADDRESS: 1410 161st St., Luverne, MN 56156

CONTACT: 507-283-6050; interpretive center: 507-283-1310 (May–September); dnr.state .mn.us/state_parks/blue_mounds

OPERATED BY: Minnesota DNR, Division of Parks and Recreation

OPEN: March–November (facilities: May–mid-October)

SITES: 71 drive-in (40 with electric), 14 cart-in, 3 tepees, 1 group

EACH SITE HAS: Open tent area, picnic table, fire ring

WHEELCHAIR ACCESS: Site 58 and 59

ASSIGNMENT: All reservable

REGISTRATION: Reserve at 866-85-PARKS (72757) or tinyurl.com/mnspreservations

FACILITIES: Restrooms, showers, vault toilets, water, sandbox

PARKING: 1 vehicle/site; at entrance to campground, on each campsite loop, and at cart-in camp area

FEES: $21/night, $17/night off-season, $29/ night electric sites, $25/night electric sites off-season, $30/night tepee Sunday– Thursday, $35/night tepee Friday–Saturday, $7 daily permit, $35 annual permit, $8.50 reservation fee

RESTRICTIONS:

PETS: On 6-foot leash; attended at all times

QUIET HOURS: 10 p.m.–8 a.m.

FIRES: In fire rings; gathering firewood not permitted; firewood must be purchased from approved vendor

ALCOHOL: Not permitted

OTHER: 6 people/site; closed to visitors 10 p.m.–8 a.m.; fireworks and metal detectors prohibited

for site 11 specifically. To varying degrees, the other campsites at these loop heads—12, 13, and 29–31—offer similar retreats from the rest of the campground.

Campsites 49–59 in the last loop back up to a treed meadow area with grasslands beyond. Sites 58 and 59 are wheelchair accessible. The top of the third loop is at the end of the roadway into the campgrounds, so more sites line this stretch. Sites 60–73 are lined up single file along this road, with lots of space between them but little privacy—this is pretty much exclusively an RV campsite section.

The 14 cart-in sites are nestled into the woodsy edge in clusters of two and three units to a site. Carts are available at the parking lot just off the main park road. A central shelter, water source, and toilet provide the only amenities in this area. While not totally private, each site is situated in or at the edge of its own stand of oak trees. Sites 1–4 and 5–8 are close together but have the woods for partial screening. Sites 13 and 14 are screened from the trail by an old building with a vault toilet. The most private sites are those closest to the creek. These are the sites I'd go after for the most remote and uncrowded experience at Blue Mounds. Trails passing through this campground lead to Upper Mound Lake and the main campground, as well as to other trails.

The influence of the prairie and forested areas along the creek is reflected in the flora and fauna that abound here. Most striking among the wild plants is the northern variety of cactus that lives here; the small prickly pear plants add colorful spots of yellow to the landscape when they blossom in the spring. The bison herd, brought here years ago—transplants from herds in Nebraska and Minnesota (from Mankato's Sibley Park Zoo)—consists of about 30 calf-bearing-age cows. Calves are born between late April and June.

With the bird-watching, prairie wildflower viewing, and appreciating the geological lay of the land, campers at Blue Mounds will find this part of extreme southwestern Minnesota a must-visit site.

Blue Mounds State Park Campground

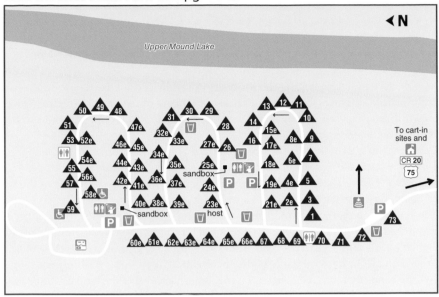

Blue Mounds State Park Cart-In Campground

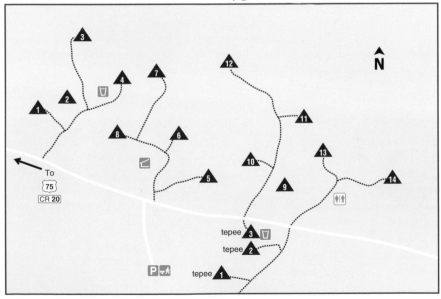

GETTING THERE

Take I-90 to Exit 12 in Luverne. Head north through Luverne on US 75 about 5 miles, then turn right (east) on CR 20 for 1 mile to the park entrance.

GPS COORDINATES: N43° 43.148' W96° 11.525'

40

Camden State Park Campgrounds

Beauty ★★★★ / Privacy ★★★★ / Spaciousness ★★ / Quiet ★★★ / Security ★★★ / Cleanliness ★★★

Enjoy rustic camping atop the steep, wooded slopes of the scenic Redwood River.

Camden State Park lies along the steep-sloped valley formed by the Redwood River as it flows through Minnesota's Coteau des Prairies ("highland of the prairie") region. The river cut down through glacial moraines to form deep, forested valleys in this otherwise flat, agricultural region of the state.

Campers can choose either the more standard and nondescript Lower Campground, with its basic open sites, or the double loops of the smaller and more rustic Upper Campground, with sites perched at the top edge of the nearly sheer, forested walls of the valley overlooking the Redwood River.

The Lower Campground layout starts out as a long roadway with sites on either side. Those on the right are laid out along the bottom of forested slopes, while the first half dozen on the left have their backs to the river. These sites are all open with a scattering of understory beneath a light forest of hardwoods. The second half of this layout forms a loop that follows the bend in the river; campsites on the eastern section of the loop continue to back up to the river, while those on the western section have the wooded slope beyond. Sites 18 and 19 are wheelchair accessible. Sites 22 and 23 are at the head of this loop and as such offer big, spacious sites. None of these sites evokes a sense of privacy, yet campsites are respectfully distanced from adjacent sites.

This campground is in the heart of the park's amenities, which include a swimming beach, a picnic area, and an amphitheater. Several hiking and mountain bike trails weave throughout this section of the park and link to additional segments that continue through the southern portions as well.

The scenic Redwood River flowing through the heart of the park

KEY INFORMATION

ADDRESS: 1897 Camden Park Road, Lynd, MN 56157

CONTACT: 507-865-4530, dnr.state.mn.us /state_parks/camden

OPERATED BY: Minnesota DNR, Division of Parks and Recreation

OPEN: Mid-March–November (water/showers: mid-May–early September or mid-October)

SITES: 80 drive-in (47 with electric), 12 equestrian, 1 group

EACH SITE HAS: Open tent area, picnic table, fire ring

WHEELCHAIR ACCESS: Sites 18 and 19

ASSIGNMENT: All reservable

REGISTRATION: Reserve at 866-85-PARKS (72757) or tinyurl.com/mnspreservations

FACILITIES: Vault toilets year-round in park, flush toilets in park office, showers mid-May–mid-October, RV sanitation station, sandbox; all wheelchair accessible

PARKING: 2 vehicles/site; across from sites 50–51 in upper campground and across from site 13 in lower campground

FEES: $23/night, $17/night off-season, $31/ night electric sites, $25/night electric sites off-season, $7 daily permit, $35 annual permit, $8.50 reservation fee

RESTRICTIONS:

PETS: On 6-foot leash; attended at all times

QUIET HOURS: 10 p.m.–8 a.m.

FIRES: In fire rings; gathering firewood not permitted; firewood must be purchased from approved vendor

ALCOHOL: Not permitted

OTHER: 6 people/site; closed to visitors 10 p.m.–8 a.m.; fireworks and metal detectors prohibited

---

The Upper Campground is located in the southern section of the park, situated on the edge of the broad, flat landscape into which this river has cut its valley. The entrance to the campground leads to two separate lobes, with campsites laid out along the contours defined by the lip of the river valley below.

The southern loop contains sites 38–63, most of which are better suited for RVs (not much for tent spaces, and many with pull-through drives). These sites are closer to the highway, suggesting a bit of traffic noise being carried across the grasslands to these open sites. Site 58 offers a level spot for tent pitching, while site 60 has a tent pad.

The northern lobe of this campground features sites 64–82. Sites 64, 66, and 67 are wooded sites in a hilly landscape with a scattered understory, which makes them fairly open but spaced farther apart than those in the Lower Campground. Some sites in the loop away from the valley edge are backed by a knoll lined with birch trees. The next several sites are small and vary in openness. Among these, site 76 is particularly appealing. Site 80 is nestled into a small cluster of oaks. These sites are close to the road, with a narrow patch of ground for pitching a tent and a backyard that drops abruptly down into the steeply wooded valley. You can sometimes see the glint of the sun reflecting off the railroad tracks that follow alongside the river. Trains passing could make for a wakeful encampment depending on your fondness for the clacking sound they make as they rumble past in the night.

My favorite site in this loop, and in the park as a whole, is 81. There's room for two small tents, and the back of the site drops immediately down over the edge toward the railroad tracks and river beyond. The slopes are covered in dense foliage, which may screen your view in the summer. Expect a flush of fall colors around this site too. Likewise, site 82 offers good tent space and a similar setting. While these are relatively small sites and close to the road, sitting at the edge of the rim facing out over the valley will give you at least a sense of lofty solitude.

Some of the activities this park offers are hiking (including a few great camera vantage points along walking bridges over the river), paddling, bicycling, swimming, trout fishing, cross-country skiing, and snowshoeing.

Camden State Park Campgrounds

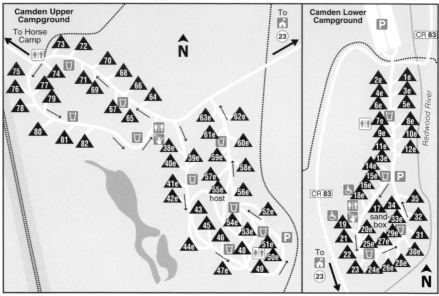

GETTING THERE

From Marshall, go 10 miles southwest on MN 23 to the park entrance on the west side of the highway.

GPS COORDINATES:
    UPPER CAMPGROUND: N44° 20.802' W95° 55.312'
    LOWER CAMPGROUND: N44° 22.096' W95° 55.456'

41

Great River Bluffs State Park Campground

Beauty ★★★★★ / Privacy ★★★★ / Spaciousness ★★★★ / Quiet ★★★★ / Security ★★★★ / Cleanliness ★★★★

Breathtaking vistas of the Mississippi Valley in Minnesota's Driftless Area will please campers.

Even if you have miles to go before you need to stop for a night of camping, treat your legs, your eyes, and your spirit to a stop-off at Great River Bluffs State Park—and then plan to camp at yet another favorite site.

Extreme southeastern Minnesota is part of what is called the Driftless Area. In geological terms that means this area was not covered in the last series of ice ages; therefore, there are no glacial deposits or drifts. Melted waters raging through these areas sculpted extremely deep and long valleys. Today, that unique topography can be experienced firsthand at Great River Bluffs State Park.

Most of the accessible areas of the park are situated along the steep and narrow ridges that fan out like the fingers on a bony hand. One finger has been developed into a modest campground and another into the group area, while other fingers reach toward the river valley below, offering breathtaking vistas of the mighty Mississippi River just north of La Crescent.

Expansive view from an overlook at the end of a short trail by the campground

KEY INFORMATION

ADDRESS: 43605 Kipp Drive, Winona, MN 55987

CONTACT: 507-643-6849; dnr.state.mn.us /state_parks/great_river_bluffs

OPERATED BY: Minnesota DNR, Division of Parks and Recreation

OPEN: May–mid-October

SITES: 31 drive-in, 4 cart-in, 5 bike-in

EACH SITE HAS: Open tent area, picnic table, fire ring

WHEELCHAIR ACCESS: Sites 6 and 8

ASSIGNMENT: All reservable, except bike-in, which are first come, first served

REGISTRATION: Reserve at 866-85-PARKS (72757) or tinyurl.com/mnspreservations

FACILITIES: Restrooms, vault toilets, water

PARKING: 1 vehicle/site (2 vehicles/site with permission); at a turnout just before entering campsite loop

FEES: $19/night, $7 daily permit, $35 annual permit, $8.50 reservation fee

RESTRICTIONS:

PETS: On 6-foot leash; attended at all times

QUIET HOURS: 10 p.m.–8 a.m.

FIRES: In fire rings; gathering firewood not permitted; firewood must be purchased from approved vendor

ALCOHOL: Not permitted

OTHER: 6 people/site; closed to visitors 10 p.m.–8 a.m.; fireworks and metal detectors prohibited

A red pine corridor, part of a scenic drive that follows the upper contours of one of many fingers, invites guests to the entrance to the campground. Because the campground lies at the opposite end from the entrance to the park, the drive in provides a wonderful opportunity to see what the entire park looks like. The park is adjacent to the Richard J. Dorer Memorial Hardwood State Forest, so it boasts its own stately stands of oak and maple as well as graceful forests of red pine.

The campground is a simple loop cut through a stand of oak, maple, birch, and aspen. What's nice about this campground is that the driveways into each site are staggered, so you don't see the campsite across the road. Like all looped configurations, those sites on the outside of the loop are more spacious and woodsy because they back up to the forest rather than to other sites. The outer sites tend to be broad rather than deep, but the dense understory of sumac, saplings, and other vegetation screens sites from one another. The sites are shady in summer and brilliantly colored in fall.

A trail curves around the eastern side of the campground and connects at each end with a trail that leads out to an overlook. A small play area for children has been developed at the base of the loop, just inside the campground across from the first site.

This is a long, narrow park with fingers stretching more than 0.5 mile out to overlooks several hundred feet above the Mississippi River. In all, eight separate vantage points overlook this driftless area. There are nearly 7 miles of hiking trails (and 9 miles of cross-country skiing trails) within the park's boundary. In fall, southeastern hardwoods are in their fiery glory.

The picnic area is off a separate spur, which forks off into two trails, each leading to its own overlook.

American Indians inhabited the area soon after glaciers retreated elsewhere, and they built mounds along many of the bluffs flanking the river. Settlers turned nearby forests into plowable lands but left the steep slopes alone. In the 1960s reforestation projects began creating plantations of introduced red pine along with native white pine, green ash, and walnut. The park also has a stand of northern white cedar, typically a colder-climate species.

Not all of the park is steep bluffs and deep ravines. There are more than 30 patches of prairie, too. Mammals and birds abound. The park is home to a diverse group of animals, including timber rattlesnakes, six-lined racerunners (a lizard), and several uncommon bird species, such as the bobolink and Henslow's sparrow.

Several miles away, down on the valley floor along US 61, Great River Bluffs State Park offers a bicycle campground with five sites virtually on the shoulder of the road. The location is quite modest, but each tent site has a table and fire ring. Noise from the highway would be intense, but at least you get a reprieve from hectic highway pedaling.

For a small, scenic campground with a unique geological history and spectacular overlooks, Great River Bluffs definitely belongs on the "best camping sites" list.

Great River Bluffs State Park Campground

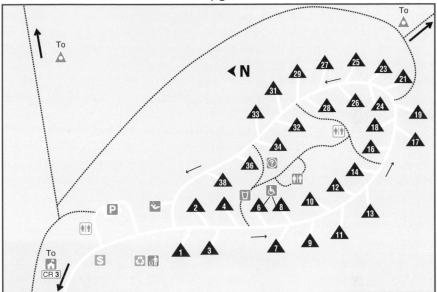

GETTING THERE

From I-90 northwest of La Crosse, take Exit 267 (CR 12), and continue north to CR 3 (CR 12 ends at the northern end of the exit ramp). Turn right (east) and follow CR 3 about 1 mile to the park entrance on the right.

GPS COORDINATES: N43° 56.383' W91° 23.088'

42

Hok-Si-La Municipal Park and Campground

Beauty ★★★ / Privacy ★★★★ / Spaciousness ★★★ / Quiet ★★★ / Security ★★★★★ / Cleanliness ★★★★

This enclosed campground is spread beneath lofty cottonwood trees on the banks of the Mississippi River, about midpoint on Lake Pepin.

Hok-Si-La earns a place in this book not only for its spacious and woodsy campsites but for a unique campground policy: When you drive up to your campsite, you'll need to unload all your gear as soon as you arrive because after 15 minutes, you have to remove your car from the campground. Vehicles must be parked outside the security gate during your stay and can only be brought back in on departure. After parking your car, hike back to your site—the farthest is about 0.5 mile from the parking lot. Camping carts/wagons are provided to help you haul gear and groceries to and from the car during your stay. Consider bringing your own cargo cart/wagon for the convenience of having it at your disposal throughout your stay. At Hok-Si-La, it's well worth the short trek.

There are four campsite groups at Hok-Si-La; three (A, B, and N) are for one or two tents, and one area (G) has six designated group sites. Groups A and B are communal spaces. The campground is divided into two relatively equal areas. The common central area is composed of a large picnic area, the caretaker's house, and a small complex of buildings: two bathhouses, a dining hall, three screened shelters, and a playground area with volleyball and basketball courts. A chapel, the camp office, and the outer perimeter parking lot take up the rest of the central core. Hok-Si-La's campsites are laid out in clusters spread

Overlook and swimming beach on the Mississippi River

photographed by Ben Threinen

KEY INFORMATION

ADDRESS: 2500 N. US 61, Lake City, MN 55041

CONTACT: 651-345-3855; hoksilapark.org

OPERATED BY: City of Lake City

OPEN: Mid-April–mid-October

SITES: 31 drive-in, 6 camper cabins, 5 group

EACH SITE HAS: Picnic table, fire ring

WHEELCHAIR ACCESS: No designated sites

ASSIGNMENT: By reservation and walk-ins

REGISTRATION: Reserve at 651-345-3855; first night's deposit required (no refunds for cancellation)

FACILITIES: Restrooms, showers, vault toilets, water

PARKING: In lots only

FEES: $26–$50/site for 2 people; $70–$90/cabin for 2 people

RESTRICTIONS:

PETS: On leash ($5/night)

QUIET HOURS: 10 p.m.–8 a.m.

FIRES: In grills or rings only; no fires on beach

ALCOHOL: Permitted

OTHER: 1–3 tents/regular sites, depending on size; 14-day stay limit; no camping on beach; swim at your own risk; closed to visitors 10 p.m.–8 a.m.

along the high banks overlooking the broad Mississippi River. The first cluster, sites A1–A13, are open, airy, and spacious. Sites A5–A7 sit at the edge of a large bank that separates the campground from the river. Bottomland trees form a forested buffer between the campers and the water. A trail leads to the swimming beach from the beach bathhouse.

Clusters B and N each have nine campsites: B is laid out just north of A. B7–B9 each offer panoramic views of Lake Pepin (a widening in the Mississippi River at Lake City). These sites are wooded, shielded by an umbrella of thick-trunked cottonwood trees.

The main campground road bisects the park, creating two areas that run parallel to the lake. Going from cluster units A and B to unit N (nine tent sites) and the group camps, trekkers walk through groves of spruce and scattered plantings of cedars, red and bur oak, maple, and white pine. The campsites and grounds throughout the entire park are very well groomed.

Both N (regular sites) and G (group sites) offer privacy. A small cluster of sites—N1, N2, N3, G0, and G2—are off by themselves at the edge of the bank above and back from the lake. The other group camps each have lots of room between them and provide at least three picnic tables, a fire ring, and piped water within a short distance. The sites are large enough to accommodate 4–10 tents in the center clearing. Sites G4 and G5 are near an embankment that drops quickly and sharply to a wooded area below.

The N sites are nicely spaced, individual sites with plenty of room between them. All sites on this side of the grounds are set into small clearings in the thick oak overstory and are very clean and secure.

The area surrounding Hok-Si-La—Lake Pepin, the lowland forests, and the river bluffs of Wisconsin across the lake—make for magical scenery. A minor downside is the constant buzz of commerce along the river and nearby US 61, a popular scenic drive. There is also train traffic along both sides of the river.

Hok-Si-La Campground offers a secure and appealing setting for both family campers and soloists. Six camper cabins are also available. Situated in the middle of the campground complex, each unit offers basic furnishings inside and a fire ring and picnic table outdoors.

It definitely offers some of the most inviting, woodsy, and hospitable camping in the state. Lake City, just 2 miles to the south, is the jumping-off point for the big boats on Lake Pepin. A boat ramp is located just inside the park with its own entrance just north of the main park road. From here canoeists and kayakers can launch a craft for miles of shore cruising.

Hok-Si-La Municipal Park and Campground

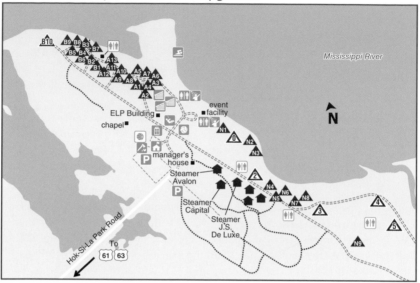

GETTING THERE

From Lake City go north 2 miles on US 61. The campground entrance is on the right.

GPS COORDINATES: N44° 28.321' W92° 17.460'

The bluffs on the Wisconsin side, across the Mississippi River

photographed by Ben Threinen

43

Minneopa State Park Campground

Beauty ★★★★ / Privacy ★★★ / Spaciousness ★★★★ / Quiet ★★★ / Security ★★★ / Cleanliness ★★★★

Glacier-formed sandstone river terraces, a bison herd, and southern Minnesota's largest waterfall add to the charm of this spot.

Minneopa State Park boasts three distinct attractions: twin waterfalls, an old gristmill, and a small herd of American bison. The waterfalls are the largest in southern Minnesota and are cut into soft sandstone, creating a beautiful, deep gorge. When the creek is flowing, they become a roaring backdrop to several trails that loop through the area, providing fantastic overlooks and photo opportunities.

This southern unit offers a pleasant city park feel with a beautifully maintained picnic area adjacent to the twin-waterfall section of this park. A short hike enables visitors to walk along and over the creek in open view of the waterfall. If it has been a dry year, don't expect to see a torrent or even a trickle. However, when the creek is flowing, this should be a spectacular sight—and sound.

The campground is north of the waterfall section, separated from it by MN 68. Each section has its official park entrance. The falls are less than 2 miles from the campground.

The northern unit of the park follows glacier-carved creekbeds created more than 15,000 years ago. The creek forming the valley emptied into the Minnesota River. That valley and the gigantic glacial boulders deposited by retreating glaciers—from bedrock more than 100 miles away—created the rock-strewn areas you see today.

The Red Fox Campground consists of 59 campsites laid out in two crescent-shaped loops. Campsites are set into a mixed forest of silver maples, cedars, and aspens. The first

The upper half of the double waterfall at Minneopa

photographed by Lisa A. Crayford

KEY INFORMATION

ADDRESS: MN 68, 0.125 mile west of 574th Avenue, Mankato, MN 56001

CONTACT: 507-386-3910; dnr.state.mn.us /state_parks/minneopa

OPERATED BY: Minnesota DNR, Division of Parks and Recreation

OPEN: Year-round (facilities: May–late October)

SITES: 59 (6 with electric), 1 camper cabin, 4 walk-in group

EACH SITE HAS: Open tent area (a few sites with tent pads), picnic table, fire ring

WHEELCHAIR ACCESS: Site A32

ASSIGNMENT: All reservable

REGISTRATION: Reserve at 866-85-PARKS (72757) or tinyurl.com/mnspreservations

FACILITIES: Restrooms, showers, vault toilets, water

PARKING: 2 vehicles/site

FEES: $21/night, $17/night off-season, $29/ night electric sites, $25/night electric sites off-season, $7 daily permit, $35 annual permit, $8.50 reservation fee

RESTRICTIONS:

PETS: On 6-foot leash; attended at all times

QUIET HOURS: 10 p.m.–8 a.m.

FIRES: In fire rings; gathering firewood not permitted; firewood must be purchased from approved vendor

ALCOHOL: Not permitted

OTHER: 6 people/site; closed to visitors 10 p.m.–8 a.m.; fireworks and metal detectors prohibited

four sites of loop A are very close to the road. As you follow loop A, the campsites on the outer perimeter are more densely wooded. Each site offers shade courtesy of the full-bodied forest. Sites inside the circle are more confined and thus less private and less spacious. All the sites have the standard-issue fire ring and picnic table. Minneopa does have a few sites with tent pads—while all others provide ample flat areas for pitching a tent. Site A32 is wheelchair accessible.

The best sites in loop A are 26 and 28—roomy, private, and under the umbrella of towering oak trees.

Loop B is similar to loop A except it's a little less shady, having fewer trees. Again, the outside of the loop, especially the higher-numbered sites, offers more room, with the surrounding forested area providing each campsite with a "backyard."

This park is a hiker and biker's holiday in summer. The valley is long and flat, with more than 2 miles of open prairie strewn with glacial boulders and accented with clumps of sumac, thistle, and scrub cedar. In the fall, wild plum trees are profuse with fruit. This area, heavily grazed by sheep before becoming park property, is now a fenced enclosure for a bison herd—a unique group whose genetic makeup is a purer strain that remains close to the herds that roamed the prairie hundreds of years ago, unaffected by cross-breeding with beef cattle. The Minnesota River Bluff Trail goes completely around the outside of the enclosure, offering hikers many chance sightings of this magnificent herd. There are about 4.5 miles of trails throughout the park.

Driving through the bison enclosure is possible throughout the year during certain hours daily (except Wednesdays). Check with the park, as these hours vary depending on conditions throughout the seasons.

The historical feature of the park is the Seppmann gristmill that sits on a ridgeline overlooking the Minnesota River valley. Built in the mid-1860s, the mill saw many prosperous years as it served the area's grain farmers. The double whammy of a damaging lightning strike followed a few years later by a debilitating tornado finally closed the mill. The vista from the mill ridge is breathtaking, especially when the valley is awash in fall color.

Minneopa's history includes a time when a local band of American Indians, called the Tribe of Sixes because they tended to build their dwellings in clusters of six, settled in the area of the park. Later this area was supposed to become a resort, but the Civil War and Dakota War of 1862 interfered with its completion.

The oak savanna sections of the park are home to bluebirds, bobolinks, and woodpeckers. Garter and bull snakes are frequent slitherers there too—neither are venomous.

Bring the cameras, fishing poles, binoculars, and a good pair of hiking shoes—you'll put them all to good use when camping at Minneopa.

Minneopa State Park Campground

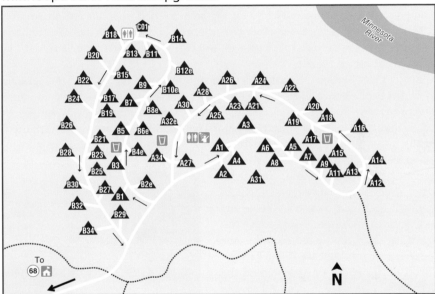

GETTING THERE

From Mankato go 3 miles west on US 169 to MN 68. Go right (west) on MN 68 and drive 1.5 miles to the northern park entrance and the campground. To get to the falls, continue on US 169 past MN 68 to CR 69, and go west 1.7 miles to the park entrance on the left. Shortcut from the campgrounds to the falls: Head back toward Mankato on MN 68, go 0.1 mile, and turn right onto CR 117. Go south 0.5 mile to the intersection with CR 69, and turn west to the falls entrance, about 0.3 mile on CR 69.

GPS COORDINATES: N44° 9.531' W94° 5.259'

Myre–Big Island State Park Campgrounds

Beauty ★★★ / Privacy ★★ / Spaciousness ★★★ / Quiet ★★★ / Security ★★★ / Cleanliness ★★★★

This island of natural amenities lies on the flat farmland along the Minnesota–Iowa border.

To hear archaeologists tell it, no sooner did the last glaciation of the most recent ice age retreat from this part of southern Minnesota than the indigenous people began settling around the lakes in this region. After 9,000 years, the Myre–Big Island area—now a state park—and the adjoining Albert Lea Lake form a recreational oasis in this otherwise agricultural area so close to the Iowa border.

Campers can thank Mother Nature for the lakes formed when the ice left and for the other features carved, gouged, and otherwise imprinted in this glacial moraine topography. Those water basins encouraged plant growth, and big-woods forests soon flanked the lakes. This, in turn, attracted wildlife.

When humans became motivated by the economics of homesteading and agriculture, many of these areas either disappeared entirely or were severely cut back in area (but were at least preserved). The park was called Big Island State Park until 1953 when Myre was added to the name in honor of state Senator Helmer Myre, whose conservation efforts saved the forests covering the island. This park also owes its preservation in part to the efforts in 1947 of amateur archaeologist and conservationist Owen Johnson. The small park he advocated for has increased tenfold into a nearly 1,600-acre park today. Remnants of oak savanna, northern hardwoods, and wetlands have all been preserved within the boundaries of Myre–Big Island State Park.

Two campgrounds—one situated on the western shore of a small inlet on Albert Lea Lake and another on Big Island—offer campers many opportunities to enjoy miles of hiking and biking trails and paddle sports out on the lake.

Situated just inside the park, White Fox Campground is the larger of the two grounds, with almost 60 sites. Sites 37–50 look like a large picnic area, complete with one fire ring and one shade tree per campsite. Sites 52 and 53 have a buffer of shrubbery between them, providing a bit more space than other sites in this loop. All the sites in the 60–63 and 67 (wheelchair accessible) grouping are exposed, not private at all. As the loop continues around, some understory begins to appear,

photographed by Bill Howe

Many paddling opportunities at Albert Lea Lakes and the Shell Rock River

KEY INFORMATION

ADDRESS: 19499 780th Ave., Albert Lea, MN 56007

CONTACT: 507-668-7060; dnr.state.mn.us /state_parks/myre_big_island

OPERATED BY: Minnesota DNR, Division of Parks and Recreation

OPEN: Year-round (facilities: May–mid-October)

SITES: 92 drive-in (32 with electric), 4 walk-in (or canoe-in or bike-in), 1 wall tent (seasonal), 1 camper cabin, 2 group

EACH SITE HAS: Open tent area (tent pads at all nonelectric sites at Big Island Campground), picnic table, fire ring

WHEELCHAIR ACCESS: Site 67

ASSIGNMENT: All reservable

REGISTRATION: Reserve at 866-85-PARKS (72757) or tinyurl.com/mnspreservations

FACILITIES: Restrooms, showers, vault toilets, water

PARKING: 2 vehicles/site; backpack parking at White Fox; visitor parking at Big Island

FEES: $21/night, $17/night off-season, $29/ night electric sites, $25/night electric sites off-season, $30/night wall tent Sunday– Thursday, $35/night wall tent Friday– Saturday, $7 daily permit, $35 annual permit, $8.50 reservation fee

---

RESTRICTIONS:

PETS: On 6-foot leash; attended at all times

QUIET HOURS: 10 p.m.–8 a.m.

FIRES: In fire rings; gathering firewood not permitted; firewood must be purchased from approved vendor

ALCOHOL: Not permitted

OTHER: 6 people/site; closed to visitors 10 p.m.–8 a.m.; fireworks and metal detectors prohibited

affording some privacy. By the time the loop returns to the main road, the view from the sites opens up to the grassy savanna again.

The Big Island Campsite is situated on Big Island and looks southwest across Albert Lea Lake. The island is actually a peninsula now, connected to the mainland by a narrow causeway. Trees are bigger as you approach the island, the characteristic species being cottonwoods, maples, and old-growth basswoods.

Campsites are very spacious and cut into the forest under a spreading canopy of hardwoods. Mature maples shade those situated in the inner loop. These sites look out onto the lake—and their long driveways may put tent campers in competition with RV users for these prime spots.

All the sites in this campground have defined pads for pitching tents. Toward the southern end of the second loop, where sites 21–35 are located, sites are more wooded, particularly 22 and 23, which back up to the woods and have more overstory than other sites in the loop. Another preferred group of tent sites is 4–7, which are also set back into the woods. Many of these sites are long and narrow with a modest understory between each one.

There are also two large group camps and several backpack-camping sites in the park, accessible from one of the hiking trails in the northern area of the park.

The best features of Myre–Big Island are the stands of mature trees (remember, this is in the heart of flat farm county) and the cluster of wetlands throughout the prairie areas. These marshy areas are a showcase of pitcher plants, bottle gentians, and wild irises—not to mention a profusion of cattails. Several restoration projects are under way in the park.

Quiet and patient wildlife viewers may be rewarded with sightings of white-tailed deer, raccoons, and even a few bat species. This park is one of the best bird-viewing areas in southern Minnesota; the list includes American kestrel, great horned owl, American bittern, wood duck, pileated woodpecker, and the especially graceful white pelican, with its 6-foot wingspan.

Just beyond the country park setting of the picnic area on the northern end of Big Island is a boat launch (and fishing pier) that gets you out onto the lake, offering miles of shoreline to explore. The 16 miles of land-based trails connect the state park routes with the paved Blazing Star State Trail west to Albert Lea. Plans are also under way to continue the trail east from the northern edge of the park. Also, the Shell Rock River State Water Trail flows south out of Albert Lea Lake, offering paddlers miles of scenic southern Minnesota countryside along the way to the Iowa border and beyond. The proximity of the water trail to the state park campsite makes this an especially appealing campground.

Myre–Big Island State Park is one of only a few places to camp in south-central Minnesota. Its proximity to the main interstate and to Iowa from the south, along with its easy access from the Twin Cities, makes it a great campground. Activities also include fishing, and canoes, kayaks, paddleboards, and snowshoes are available for rent.

Myre–Big Island State Park Campgrounds

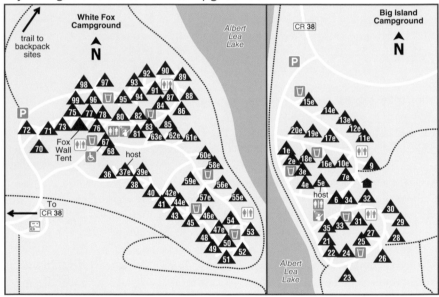

GETTING THERE

Located 3 miles southeast of Albert Lea on CR 38. Take Exit 11 (CR 46) from I-35 east to CR 38, then turn right (south) to the park entrance straight ahead. Good signage directs you to the park from either I-35 or I-90.

GPS COORDINATES:
WHITE FOX: N43° 38.070' W93° 18.208'
BIG ISLAND: N43° 37.468' W93° 17.612'

45

Nerstrand–Big Woods State Park Campground

Beauty ★★★ / Privacy ★★★★ / Spaciousness ★★★★★ / Quiet ★★★★ / Security ★★★ / Cleanliness ★★★★

The best sites are at the walk-in campground, with great hiking along trails that lead to a waterfall.

If you are deciding where to camp to enjoy rich fall color, look no further than Nerstrand–Big Woods State Park. I love this park, with its rich, warm maple reds and golds; the striking glens of brilliant fall leaves; and winding, climbing trails underneath a big-woods canopy.

That said, I must admit that the best campsites in this park are few and far between—in the walk-in section of the park. The main camping area is a typical state park pattern of loop and cutout campsites. The individual sites are, for the most part, set a fair distance apart but with no understory to block views—the entire campground is too open for my taste. However, sites 20, 22, and 23, outside the loop, have more space and privacy and back up to the forest.

The campground loop is bisected laterally by a road offering even more spacious, open sites—this is where the RVs herd. It is pretty in the campground, thanks to the towering basswoods, red oaks, and maples that make up the mature stand of forest from which the area was developed. A nice trail leads from between sites 18 and 20 to several trail intersections and is less than 0.5 mile from the park's picturesque waterfall.

Hidden Falls, a short distance from the main campground

photographed by Lisa A. Crayford

KEY INFORMATION

ADDRESS: 9700 170th St. E, Nerstrand, MN 55053

CONTACT: 507-384-6140; dnr.state.mn.us /state_parks/nerstrand_big_woods

OPERATED BY: Minnesota DNR, Division of Parks and Recreation

OPEN: April–mid-October (facilities: May–mid-October)

SITES: 51 drive-in (26 with electric), 4 walk-in, 3 group

EACH SITE HAS: Open tent area, picnic table, fire ring

WHEELCHAIR ACCESS: Sites 33 and 44

ASSIGNMENT: All reservable

REGISTRATION: Reserve at 866-85-PARKS (72757) or tinyurl.com/mnspreservations

FACILITIES: Restroom, showers, vault toilets, water

PARKING: 1 vehicle/site; at the group camping area, 0.3 mile west of the main park entrance; parking spur for each walk-in site

FEES: $23/night, $17/night off-season, $31/ night electric sites, $25/night electric sites off-season, $7 daily permit, $35 annual permit, $8.50 reservation fee

RESTRICTIONS:

PETS: On 6-foot leash; attended at all times

QUIET HOURS: 10 p.m.–8 a.m.

FIRES: In fire rings; gathering firewood not permitted; firewood must be purchased from approved vendor

ALCOHOL: Not permitted

OTHER: 6 people/site; closed to visitors 10 p.m.–8 a.m.; fireworks and metal detectors prohibited

---

The best camping is available at the four walk-in tent sites across from the group sites. There's the trade-off: If the group camp is filled with a noisy group, campers across the road are going to suffer. Otherwise, the spaciousness of each site and the distance between sites—all of which are nicely screened by dense understory—make these worth seeking.

Walk-in distances vary from 12 yards or so to perhaps 40 yards from the parking spurs. The sites themselves are at least 40–50 yards apart and feature basic amenities such as a fire ring and a picnic table. I camped here late one fall and caution you to keep all your food secure: I had a raccoon snatch a carton of milk right off the picnic table in the time it took me to retrieve something from my tent, a mere 20 feet away.

Sites 1 and 4 are the farthest from their neighbors, and sites 2 and 3 are fairly close together by walk-in standards. Each campsite backs up to the mature forest of maples and oaks. A trailhead at the end of the parking lot connects to all the routes in the park. At the other end of the lot are trails for snowshoeing and snowmobiling in winter. Another trail parallels the road and leads campers back to the park's entrance.

Each walk-in site has a parking spur, and you'll find water and vault toilets beyond the parking lot.

Regardless of the time of year, Nerstrand–Big Woods offers great trails through stately stands of trees and in some areas along exposed rock that hints at the park's geological history. The forests are all that remains of the more than 5,000 acres of large hardwoods that were common to the area when it was first settled by nonnatives. In fact, it was these insightful homesteaders who realized the value of these forests and managed to secure almost 300 acres of the Big Woods for posterity.

Geologically, the park lies on two horizontal strata laid down by recent glaciation. One layer is glacial drift that is about 150 feet thick and overlies Platteville limestone (the floor of an Ordovician sea almost 500 million years ago). The upper, more claylike layer continues to erode, exposing the limestone. There are several places in the park where this extreme erosion is most evident, such as at Hidden Falls, where the creek has slowly but steadily worn away the upper layers, creating a shelf 4 yards high by 30 yards wide. Water flowing over this shelf continues to cut into the sublayers, constantly digging the pool beneath the falls. Exposed rock along sections of the Prairie Creek bottoms is yet more evidence of the abrasive action of the water on this layer.

The network of looped trails off the campgrounds can be combined to create hikes varying in length and changes in elevation that lead you back to the campground. Fortunately, all these routes intersect close to Hidden Falls, so each trail takes you by this geological wonder.

Saving this camping opportunity until autumn may mean a dry creek and no waterfall, but the reds and golds of the forest will more than make up for it. Other amenities include an interpretive center, a picnic area, and cross-country ski trails (note that these are no longer groomed).

Nerstrand–Big Woods State Park Campground

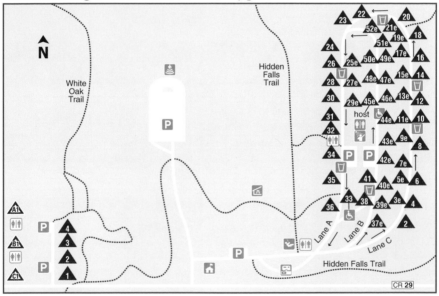

GETTING THERE

From I-35 take Exit 56 at Faribault. Take MN 60 east 2.2 miles to Third Street NE, and turn left. In 0.6 mile, veer left (northeast) on CR 20 (Cannon City Boulevard) and go 4 miles to Cannon City. Take a right (north) onto CR 30 and go 1.4 miles to the intersection with CR 88 (170th Street East). Continue onto CR 88 and go about 4 miles to the park entrance on the left.

GPS COORDINATES: N44° 20.550' W93° 6.227'

46

⚘ Rice Lake State Park Campgrounds

Beauty ★★★ / Privacy ★★★★ / Spaciousness ★★★★★ / Quiet ★★★ / Security ★★★ / Cleanliness ★★★

A choice remote campground is set in a park featuring geological and cultural history and wonderful seasonal bird-watching.

This is another state park where the remote, walk-in campsites steal the show from the semimodern arrangement developed for the park. The five walk-ins are aligned along a gravel road that takes off north from the main campground loop, and each has a picnic table and fire pit. Toilets are at the entrance to this area, and water is available 0.25 mile away at the main campground.

Not to be confused with the walk-in sites, there are also four cart-in campsites located along the shore of Rice Lake, just south of the boat ramp and about 0.25 mile west of the main campground. There's a parking area on the park road, just east of the access trail to these rustic sites.

A short walk to campsites within the lush forest

KEY INFORMATION

ADDRESS: 8485 Rose St., Owatonna, MN 55060

CONTACT: 507-414-6190; dnr.state.mn.us /state_parks/rice_lake

OPERATED BY: Minnesota DNR, Division of Parks and Recreation

OPEN: April–mid-October (facilities: May–mid-October)

SITES: 40 drive-in (18 with electric), 5 walk-in, 4 cart-in, 5 canoe-in, 1 group

EACH SITE HAS: Open tent area, picnic table, fire ring

WHEELCHAIR ACCESS: Sites A20, B11, and B17

ASSIGNMENT: All reservable

REGISTRATION: Reserve at 866-85-PARKS (72757) or tinyurl.com/mnspreservations

FACILITIES: Restroom, showers, toilets, boat ramp

PARKING: 1 vehicle/site (2 vehicles/site with permission); parking lots near walk-in and cart-in sites

FEES: $21/night, $17/night off-season, $29/ night electric sites, $25/night electric sites off-season, $$7 daily permit, $35 annual permit, $8.50 reservation fee

---

RESTRICTIONS:

PETS: On 6-foot leash; attended at all times

QUIET HOURS: 10 p.m.–8 a.m.

FIRES: In fire rings; gathering firewood not permitted; firewood must be purchased from approved vendor

ALCOHOL: Not permitted

OTHER: 6 people/site; closed to visitors 10 p.m.–8 a.m.; fireworks and metal detectors prohibited

My field notes indicate "great place to camp" and "private/secluded" in reference to the walk-in sites. These are the kinds of areas where I like to camp. The overstory of oak and basswood gives them a deep-woods feel, and the distance between spacious sites is a real advantage. The walk-in sites are connected to all trail systems and, being on the far end of the campground development, offer immediate access to the undeveloped areas networked by trails throughout the park's eastern half.

The semimodern campground is nestled into tall stands of oaks, basswoods, and maples to give it a solid big-woods feel. There is also a mature understory of younger trees that separates sites and offers some privacy in the two campsite loops.

Loop A has fully wooded sites featuring the basic Department of Natural Resources furnishings of picnic table, fire ring, tent pad, and parking space (wheelchair-accessible site A20 has hard-packed gravel instead of a tent pad). Sites are spacious and laid out with ample room to arrange a nice camp area. There is little underbrush between the sites, but the younger trees and saplings that make up the understory provide visual diffusion between one campsite and the next. If the walk-ins are full, loop A, especially those sites on the outer part of the loop, would be a good second choice.

Loop B is configured like loop A. An additional buffer of underbrush blocks direct views into other sites. This is a good thing because the sites in loop B are closer together and less spacious. That being said, loop B seems to be the lane of choice for larger RVs as well— another reason to consider loop A as a backup if the walk-ins are full.

Even though there is a "big tree" feel about the landscape surrounding Rice Lake, it is actually situated in what used to be the southern oak barrens that spread from Iowa all the way up to the Twin Cities. These oak barrens define the line between the western prairies and the hardwood forests closer to the Mississippi Valley.

Geologically, this area used to be part of a great sea. Thick bedrock deposited 500 million years ago forms its foundation. The most recent glaciation caused many changes, including large drainage systems from melting ice that worked their way to the even larger cuts made by the prehistoric Mississippi to the east. Rice Lake actually sits on a divide that sent waters east and west. If it were drained today, ancient channels carved by that melting ice would be visible on the lake's bottom. Water also played a role in the area's more recent history when local creeks were dammed in attempts to start a water-powered gristmill operation.

For the more adventurous and solitude-seeking canoe camper, there are a few canoe-in campsites located across the lake from the main campground. Astute birders will realize the strategic position of Rice Lake along regional flyways. Its marshes, lake, and meadow provide ideal habitats for protection and rest—not to mention nesting sites for a large number of migrating waterfowl. The mature forests have attracted seven Minnesota species of woodpeckers, including the largest of the lot—the pileated woodpecker (nature trivia: the pileated woodpecker was the inspiration for the famous cartoon character Woody Woodpecker). Look for swans, Canada geese, and a variety of surface-feeding ducks throughout the spring.

If your primary activity while camping is enjoying nature, paddling (canoe and kayak rentals available), hiking, or just hanging out away from the congestion, Rice Lake may be your answer.

Rice Lake State Park Campgrounds

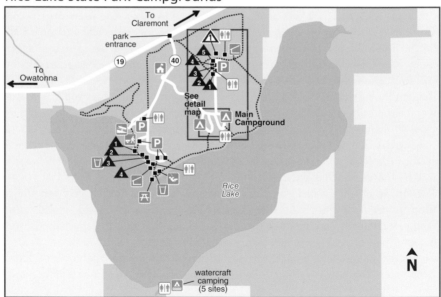

Rice Lake State Park Campground Detail

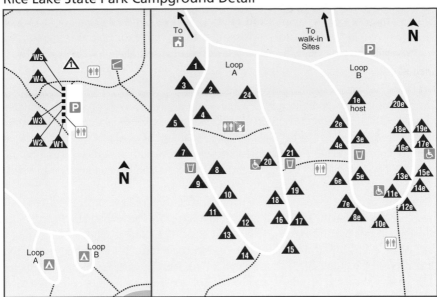

GETTING THERE

From Owatonna go about 8 miles east on CR 19 (Rose Street) to the park entrance on the right.

GPS COORDINATES: N44° 5.357' W93° 3.649'

47

⚴ Sakatah Lake State Park Campground

Beauty ★★★ / Privacy ★★★★ / Spaciousness ★★★★ / Quiet ★★★★ / Security ★★★ / Cleanliness ★★★★

Take a tranquil hike over the hills, through lush forests, and along a wide spot in the Cannon River.

My introduction to Sakatah State Park came while doing research on another guidebook for Menasha Ridge Press: *60 Hikes Within 60 Miles: Minneapolis and St. Paul.* As on the first visit, I was again struck by the lushness of this area along the banks of the Cannon River in southern Minnesota. From a forestry perspective, the Sakatah area delineates a boundary between the big-woods forest of south-central Minnesota and the oak barrens and savanna areas to the south.

Dense forests of mature oaks in the uplands and cottonwoods in the lower areas provide the overstory for an equally lush array of ground foliage. This lushness helps keep campsites private even in this park of extra-spacious tent sites. The campground is made up of four loops, two on each side of the main campground road. Sites 1–15 are laid out in typical fashion: driveway, picnic table, and fire ring. The understory is dense but not as mature as in other areas of the park, yet sites are quiet and isolated from each other compared to many other campgrounds in the state. Sites 9 and 14 have tent pads.

As in most loop configurations, the campsites outside the circle are more spread out. The dense understory is shaded by maple and ash, with sumac accenting the underbrush. There is a sense of privacy even in this young forest.

A portion of the Sakatah Singing Hills State Trail that crosses through the heart of the park

KEY INFORMATION

ADDRESS: 50499 Sakatah Lake State Park Road, Waterville, MN 56096

CONTACT: 507-362-4438; dnr.state.mn.us/state_parks/sakatah_lake

OPERATED BY: Minnesota DNR, Division of Parks and Recreation

OPEN: April–mid-October (facilities: May–mid-October)

SITES: 62 drive-in (14 with electric), 5 bike-in, 1 camper cabin, 2 group

EACH SITE HAS: Open tent area (8 sites have tent pads), picnic table, fire ring

WHEELCHAIR ACCESS: Sites 32 and 50

ASSIGNMENT: All reservable, except bike-in, which are first come, first served

REGISTRATION: Reserve at 866-85-PARKS (72757) or tinyurl.com/mnspreservations

FACILITIES: Restroom, showers, vault toilets, water

PARKING: 1 vehicle/site; at visitor center and picnic area

FEES: $23/night, $17/night off-season, $31/night electric sites, $25/night electric sites off-season, $7 daily permit, $35 annual permit, $8.50 reservation fee

---

RESTRICTIONS:

PETS: On 6-foot leash; attended at all times

QUIET HOURS: 10 p.m.–8 a.m.

FIRES: In fire rings; gathering firewood not permitted; firewood must be purchased from approved vendor

ALCOHOL: Not permitted

OTHER: 6 people/site; closed to visitors 10 p.m.–8 a.m.; fireworks and metal detectors prohibited

---

Among sites 16–33 (site 32 is wheelchair accessible; site 26 has a tent pad), the outside loop locations are the best choices in the second loop of campsites. These sites, in general, are a bit bigger, and the broad understory between sites adds to the lushness. The forest of oaks and maples is more mature in this loop.

Bigger still are the sites along the third loop of campsites, numbered 34–47. The road through this section has more twists, but the bigger sites lure RVs. Still, the tent camper will find sites far enough apart, and the serpentine road winding over the hilly terrain enough to separate these sites from others. Sites 40, 41, 42, and 47 have tent pads, while others have open areas for tent pitching. Site 40 is especially nice as it sits on the outside of its campground loop, offering more space and privacy than other sites.

The last loop has quiet and spacious staggered campsites (site 50 is wheelchair accessible). A hiking trail that cuts between sites 16 and 18 in the second loop (a shortcut to the state trail) leaves the campground again between sites 54 and 56 on its way to the nearby lake. Sites 59 and 62 have tent pads.

This park provides trails for people on the move. Formed by glacial activity almost 15,000 years ago, the hills—some more than 400 feet high—are covered with lush stands of oak, basswood, maple, and ash, creating a peaceful wooded retreat. The glaciers also left behind large chunks of ice, some so big that when they melted they created wide lakes in the otherwise narrow river.

Humankind has recorded its history in this park as well. First the Wahpekute of the Dakota Nation inhabited the area and named it Sakatah, which translates into "singing hills." Because of the dense, big woods throughout this area, the Cannon and other rivers became vital water routes for travel between this part of Minnesota and Wisconsin. Trading posts were established, and the Wahpekute developed a village site between the two lakes in the park.

In more recent history, and to the ultimate delight of hikers and bicyclists, the Cannon Valley Company developed a railroad between Faribault and Mankato. Later, as a part of the Chicago and Northwestern Railroad, that portion of the route was abandoned, and the railroad bed was converted into the present-day segment of the Sakatah Singing Hills State Trail. A Big Woods Loop Trail west of the campground gives hikers a chance to trek through stands of mature hardwoods typical of the Big Woods era of south-central Minnesota.

Ambitious bicyclists can pedal through the forests and grasslands to Faribault, 14 miles east, or to Mankato, 22 miles west.

Campers will have many opportunities to view wildlife, particularly at the transitions between dense forest and oak-savanna prairie. Deer, two varieties of foxes, raccoons, and muskrats all reside within the park. It's also a wonderful place for bird-watching.

Sakatah Lake can easily keep a family of campers occupied for a weekend or longer, depending on the amount of hiking they enjoy. It will be equally pleasant for those who just want to relax under the dense canopy of southern Minnesota's hardwood forest.

One word of concern: Sakatah is a very shallow lake and therefore is prone to dense algae blooms in midsummer that can produce unpleasant odors. There is no swimming beach, and the Department of Natural Resources recommends visiting Sakatah in spring, early summer, or fall—avoiding the lake during hot August, when the algae bloom is typically at its peak.

Sakatah Lake State Park Campground

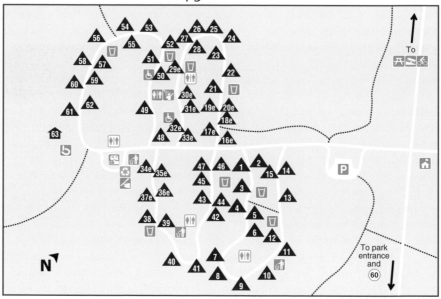

GETTING THERE

The park entrance is on MN 60, 15 miles west of Faribault or 1 mile east of Waterville.

GPS COORDINATES: N44° 13.209' W93° 32.033'

48

Split Rock Creek State Park Campground

Beauty ★★★ / Privacy ★★★ / Spaciousness ★★★★ / Quiet ★★★ / Security ★★★ / Cleanliness ★★★★★

A dam built across a tiny creek created one of the biggest recreational getaways in this treeless, grassy expanse of Minnesota.

The area around Split Rock Creek is typical of the southwestern area of Minnesota—cornfields and farm country. Split Rock Creek State Park is a quaint oasis of forest and lake smack-dab in the middle of this agricultural flatland. The locals use this park for wonderfully relaxing evenings of fishing and hiking alongside the fortunate campers who happen across this spot.

Split Rock Creek is unique in that it is part of a portion of southwestern Minnesota called the Coteau des Prairies—a section of the state whose waters flow not into the Mississippi River but to the west and into the Missouri River. This otherwise insignificant creek flowed uninterrupted through the treeless prairie until 1938, when a dam was built where it flows under County Road 20 today. Since then it has become one of the most popular recreation areas in Pipestone County.

Fishing pier on Split Rock Lake

KEY INFORMATION

ADDRESS: 336 50th Ave., Jasper, MN 56144

CONTACT: 507-348-7908; dnr.state.mn.us /state_parks/split_rock_creek

OPERATED BY: Minnesota DNR, Division of Parks and Recreation

OPEN: April–mid-October (facilities: May–mid-October)

SITES: 28 drive-in (21 with electric), 6 walk-in, 1 group

EACH SITE HAS: Open tent area, picnic table, fire ring

WHEELCHAIR ACCESS: Sites 3, 5–7, 10–12, 14–17, and 19

ASSIGNMENT: All reservable

REGISTRATION: Reserve at 866-85-PARKS (72757) or tinyurl.com/mnspreservations

FACILITIES: Restrooms, showers, vault toilets, water

PARKING: 1 vehicle/site; parking area along spur loop across from walk-in sites A–F

FEES: $21/night, $17/night off-season, $29/ night electric sites, $25/night electric sites off-season, $7 daily permit, $35 annual permit, $8.50 reservation fee

RESTRICTIONS:

PETS: On 6-foot leash; attended at all times

QUIET HOURS: 10 p.m.–8 a.m.

FIRES: In fire rings; gathering firewood not permitted; firewood must be purchased from approved vendor

ALCOHOL: Not permitted

OTHER: 6 people/site; closed to visitors 10 p.m.–8 a.m.; fireworks and metal detectors prohibited

On entering the park, campers may be mildly seduced by the peaceful setting of the lake formed by that dam. The tranquility of the site is further enhanced by the modest forest that spreads from the shoreline. This grove of ash and elm trees was planted 80 years ago by park developers. The road into the campsites follows the western shore of Split Rock Lake toward the short campground loops at the end of the road.

One small but significant natural attraction of this park, besides the pastoral lake, is the small, upward sloping hill on the left just before you enter the campground loop. Those seemingly unremarkable grasses and plants are growing on a hillside that has never seen the blade of a plow and never been scarred by a farmer's furrow. It remains in its original state—a lone remnant of what thousands of square miles of Midwest prairie looked like less than a few centuries ago. This may indeed be the most important feature of this park!

The oblong loop of the campground road offers 28 sites plus a spur loop with 6 more campsites. The first two sites on the right, 2 and 4, are choice locations for camping near the lake. A basic picnic table, fire ring, and gravel driveway—standard issue for the Department of Natural Resources—make up the sites' amenities. The lake in the background makes these more appealing than sites in the inner loop. The rest of the sites on the main loop are smallish, keyhole sites fairly close to the road. Those outside the road loop are more spacious and private, albeit with a fairly scant understory. Campsites 3, 5, 6, 7, and 10 are wheelchair accessible. Sites 11–20 (sites 11, 12, 14–17, and 19 are wheelchair accessible) at the upper end of the loop and the inside sites toward the end (odd numbers 21–27) all have electricity, so expect to see machinery camped at these. When full, this campground bustles with campers in close proximity to each other.

A small looped spur off to the right immediately after site 6 leads to walk-in campsites A–F. These are the most private sites, and all are on the lake side of the campground area. Camp here if you can. It's a small enough park that you are still close to all the attractions and amenities, including water and toilets. There's even a small playground adjacent to the parking area. The road continues beyond these sites and heads to the group camp.

Because Split Rock Creek and Lake are the only large bodies of water in this grassy sea, they are a natural draw for wildlife, especially waterfowl and other birds. Campers in the spring and fall will witness migrating swans, pelicans, and other winged visitors.

The lake teems with sunfish, walleye, and perch. A trail encircles nearly the entire lake but does not form a loop. Except for a short section at the extreme southern end, hikers can practically circumnavigate Split Rock Lake on foot as well as by water. Bordering the lake along the eastern shore are reeds, and the western edges are forested.

Pipestone National Monument is only 8.5 miles north of Split Rock Creek. American Indians would travel to this area from hundreds of miles away to cut the red clay from the earth to make bowls for their peace pipes and other ceremonial items. An interpretive trail winds through the prairie and rock outcrops, and past the open, active mine pits.

Split Rock Creek State Park Campground

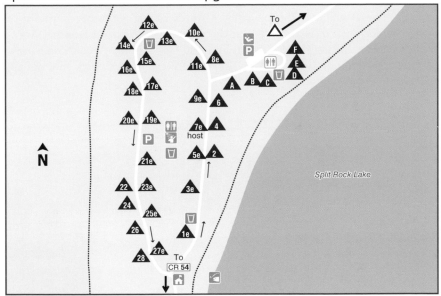

GETTING THERE

From Pipestone at the intersection of MN 30 and MN 23, go south about 6.7 miles on MN 23 to CR 2 (Judd Street) in Ihlen. Turn left (east) onto CR 2, and then in 0.2 mile turn right (south) onto CR 20. Go south on CR 20 about 0.8 mile to the park entrance on the left.

From I-90 east of Sioux Falls, take Exit 12 and turn north onto US 75 at Luverne; go approximately 14 miles to CR 2. Turn left (west) and go 5 miles to CR 20 at Ihlen; then turn left (south) on CR 20 and go about 0.8 mile to the park entrance on the left.

GPS COORDINATES: N43° 54.017' W96° 21.966'

49

⚠ Upper Sioux Agency State Park Campground

Beauty ★★★ / Privacy ★★ / Spaciousness ★★★ / Quiet ★★★ / Security ★★★★ / Cleanliness ★★★★

For diverse landscapes and important history, this park provides a well-rounded camping experience—and gives you the opportunity to camp in a tepee.

The park's name emphasizes its prominence as a historic site. The Treaty of Traverse Des Sioux forced the Dakota to resettle from Iowa to a reservation laid out along the Minnesota River. The Upper Sioux Agency (originally called the Yellow Medicine Agency after the river that flows nearby) was built to administer that treaty. The agency was destroyed during the Dakota War of 1862.

History aside, the natural setting of the park is an attraction all its own. Situated on a plateau of glacial moraine, the landscape features rolling, grass-covered hills; dense hardwood forests with majestic bur oaks; the meandering Yellow Medicine River; and large patches of prairie grasslands. The area around Upper Sioux Agency State Park features some of the oldest exposed rock on Earth. Granite and gneiss rock outcrops appear throughout the region.

One of three authentic camping tepees in the campground loop

KEY INFORMATION

ADDRESS: 5908 MN 67, Granite Falls, MN 56241

CONTACT: 320-564-4777; dnr.state.mn.us /state_parks/upper_sioux_agency

OPERATED BY: Minnesota DNR, Division of Parks and Recreation

OPEN: April–October (facilities: May–mid-October)

SITES: 28 drive-in (14 with electric), 3 tepees, 3 walk-in, 7 rustic drive-to (at Riverside), 36 equestrian

EACH SITE HAS: Open tent area, picnic table, fire ring

WHEELCHAIR ACCESS: No designated sites

ASSIGNMENT: All reservable

REGISTRATION: Reserve at 866-85-PARKS (72757) or tinyurl.com/mnspreservations

FACILITIES: Restroom, showers, water, boat ramp, electricity (2 sites with 50 amps)

PARKING: 2 vehicles/site; parking area between sites 1 and 5 for walk-in

FEES: $21/night, $17/night off-season, $29/ night electric sites, $23/night electric sites off-season, $30/night tepee Sunday– Thursday, $35/night tepee Friday–Saturday, $7 daily permit, $35 annual permit, $8.50 reservation fee

---

RESTRICTIONS:

PETS: On 6-foot leash; attended at all times

QUIET HOURS: 10 p.m.–8 a.m.

FIRES: In fire rings; gathering firewood not permitted; firewood must be purchased from approved vendor

ALCOHOL: Not permitted

OTHER: 6 people/site; closed to visitors 10 p.m.–8 a.m.; fireworks and metal detectors prohibited

---

The first time I camped here, I enjoyed the haunting howl of coyotes as a full moon rose beyond the bluffs of the Minnesota River, which defines the eastern edge of the park. The campground is nestled into a prairie meadow bordered by trees that extend to the banks of the nearby Yellow Medicine River, which flows just beyond the campground loop. Three tepees, their canvas skins gleaming in the prairie sun, dominate the scene as you enter the campground.

Site 1 is an open, grassy site right on the edge of the trees that serve as the backdrop for all the sites along this part of the loop. Sites 2–4 are walk-ins accessible from a trail from a parking lot just beyond site 1. They are in a mature stand of trees and overlook the river. Site 5 is open and backed by trees. Site 6 is one of three tepee sites—more on these later. Sites 7–10 are fairly open with a scattering of trees on the river side and open grassy meadows on the inside of the loop.

Site 11 is one of those sites where the driveway is as wide as the campsite, making it highly visible to passersby. Site 12 is located in a grassy area that looks like it could stay wet after a good rain. Site 13 is also open but has a nice backdrop of trees to give it a little more appeal. Site 14 is an open meadow site. The campground road forks just after sites 13 and 14. The left fork leads on through sites 15–19, all of which are very open, exposed, and tree-less. Site 18 is huge! These are the sites most likely to be taken by the larger RVs.

The right fork in the road circles out into another section of the grassland and features the other two tepees. These occupy sites 24 and 26. The 18-foot diameter shelters were erected in the park in 1999. Covered in white canvas instead of the traditional buffalo hide and resting just above the ground on a cedar platform, these tepees, styled after the Plains Indian homes, are a summerlong structure in the park.

The tepees are full-size, functional shelters complete with all the flaps, folds, and structural integrity of an authentic tepee. You should bring a cot or good mattress because they all have wood floors. They are wheelchair accessible too. A park brochure offers tips on how to manipulate vent flaps and other intricacies of tepee living.

The other sites along the outer fork of the campground loop are also spacious, open grassland sites. Site 29 is especially large and favored by the big RV rigs.

Beyond the attraction of sleeping in a tepee, the park offers 16 miles of multiuse trails (for hikers or equestrians), plus an additional 2 miles of hiking-only trails. The paths wind through meadows and grassy knolls and occasionally follow the banks of the Minnesota and Yellow Medicine Rivers in a network that stretches from one end of the park to the other.

The section of the Minnesota River that forms the northern boundary of the park provides paddlers plenty of gently flowing water for canoeing or kayaking. A river access point (Kinney Landing) just south of Granite Falls on MN 67 enables river travelers to float about 7 miles downstream to a takeout at the park. A riverside campground—popular with late-night river fishermen—offers primitive camping (water and vault toilets available) for both land-based and river-tripping campers.

Other activities include birding, paddling, hiking, and a winter sledding (or sliding) hill.

Upper Sioux Agency State Park Campground

GETTING THERE

From Granite Falls head south on MN 67 for 8 miles to the park entrance on the left. The campground road is about another mile farther, on the left just before the bridge over the Yellow Medicine River.

GPS COORDINATES: N44° 43.836' W95° 26.176'

50

⚠ Whitewater State Park Campgrounds

Beauty ★★★ / Privacy ★★★ / Spaciousness ★★★ / Quiet ★★★ / Security ★★★ / Cleanliness ★★★★

This is one of southeastern Minnesota's most popular camping parks—a classic setting rich in resources and scenic beauty.

Driving toward the entrance to Whitewater State Park, particularly from the southern access route on MN 74, one begins to experience the beauty of this area. Dense forests line the valley floors right up to the ridgetops. Occasionally, sheer walls of dolomite rock protrude through the canopy of oaks and maples. The winding road, thick woods, and towering rock extrusions all characterize this scenic section of southeastern Minnesota and are showcased beautifully within Whitewater State Park.

Now the reality check: Expect this park to be very busy between April and Labor Day. Its popularity reminds me of a classic joke famously employed by Yogi Berra about a popular restaurant: "Nobody goes there anymore. It's too crowded." It's that kind of skewed rationale that could cause some to think twice about Whitewater—it's always so darn busy!

That said, there are some options available for persistent campers or those whose appreciation for the amenities, natural and otherwise, can block out the throngs of fellow campers.

The semimodern campsites, all 119 of them, are configured within seven loops in Cedar Hill and Minneiska Campgrounds. Most of the tent camping is at Cedar Hill, with the exception of the four sites at Minneiska and four cart-in sites just south of Cedar Hill.

Sites 1–13 are laid out along the floor of the Whitewater River valley in spacious and open sites that offer back-to-back camping with little privacy. Sites 14–32 have more vegetation and overstory and thus a greater sense of privacy. Site 25 is wheelchair accessible. The sites are fairly far apart and roomy, just visually connected. Sites 33–47 and 49 are long and more open underneath but with large, tall trees above. Big and spacious, these sites are attractive to RVs as well.

Sites 48 and 50–75 (site 57 is wheelchair accessible) are smaller spots nestled into slightly taller stands of oak and maple. The campsites along the outside edge of the western side of this loop (sites 62–63, 65–67, and 69–70) are near the base of a sandstone bluff, along which runs the Middle Branch of the Whitewater River. These sites are also a bit more private. In fact, sites 62 and 63 have the added luxury of a denser understory of

Whitewater River in the campground

KEY INFORMATION

ADDRESS: 19041 MN 74, Altura, MN 55910

CONTACT: 507-312-2300, dnr.state.mn.us /state_parks/whitewater

OPERATED BY: Minnesota DNR, Division of Parks and Recreation

OPEN: Year-round (facilities: early April–mid-October)

SITES: 119 drive-in (87 with electric), 4 cart-in, 4 camper cabins, 3 primitive group

EACH SITE HAS: Picnic table, fire ring

WHEELCHAIR ACCESS: Sites 25, 57, 206, 214, 219, 228, 239, 242, and 244

ASSIGNMENT: All reservable

REGISTRATION: Reserve at 866-85-PARKS (72757) or tinyurl.com/mnspreservations

FACILITIES: Restrooms, showers, vault toilets, water, fishing pier, amphitheater

PARKING: 1 vehicle/site (2 vehicles/site with permission); parking area near walk-in sites; next to visitor center and at picnic area; at trailheads throughout park

FEES: $23/night, $17/night off-season, $31/ night electric sites, $25/night electric sites off-season, $7 daily permit, $35 annual permit, $8.50 reservation fee

---

RESTRICTIONS:

PETS: On 6-foot leash; attended at all times

QUIET HOURS: 10 p.m.–8 a.m.

FIRES: In fire rings; gathering firewood not permitted; firewood must be purchased from approved vendor

ALCOHOL: Not permitted

OTHER: 6 people/site; closed to visitors 10 p.m.–8 a.m.; fireworks and metal detectors prohibited

---

privacy-creating vegetation. An outcrop of sandstone between sites 69 and 70 offers even more privacy between those two sites. The proximity of the river adds a special touch to the appeal of these particular sites.

The cart-in sites are toward this bluffline as you move from the larger campground at Cedar Hill south. A trail off toward the bluff leads to four cart-in sites with basic amenities. Beyond these sites is the exposed dolomite bluff and the Whitewater River.

The primitive group sites across the highway from the main body of the park are big, spacious, and private. They are a good walking distance from most of the park's amenities but worth the price if you seek some distance from the city of campers across the road. The capacity of the combined primitive sites is listed as 100 campers, so these are held for organized groups, such as Scouts and church camps. Still, a family reunion could be fantastic if staged here—and the group might easily feel as though they had the place to themselves.

The newest addition to this popular southern Minnesota state park are 45 individual campsites and 3 group sites in the newly developed Minneiska Campground. Located across the highway from the park entrance, this multilooped camping area features 41 RV/tent sites in four loops and 4 tent-only campsites at the southern end of the campground. Sites 206, 214, 219, 228, and 239 (and sites 242 and 244 in the tent-only section) are wheelchair accessible. This campground is nestled near the base of the forested high bluffs that form the Whitewater River valley. The reason for this park's popularity is, as stated, the beautiful setting—but perhaps also for its reputation of no mosquitoes! Couple that with fantastic fishing and a wonderful network of hiking trails, and adventurous campers can find plenty to do here for days on end. The park's geological and cultural history is similar to that of other parks in the region, having been sculpted by receding waters and settled by American Indians and then early homesteaders. Its lush forests of oak, maple, and basswood; streams full of brown, brook, and rainbow trout; and representative flora and fauna were all treasured by regional conservationists who took action to preserve the area as a state park in 1919.

Whitewater State Park Campgrounds

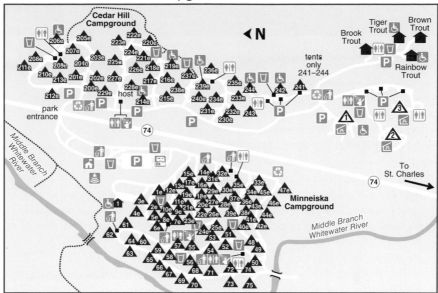

GETTING THERE

From Rochester take US 14 east to St. Charles. From St. Charles take MN 74 north about 6 miles to the park entrance.

From US 61 at Weaver take MN 74 south. The park entrance is 3 miles south of Elba on the right.

GPS COORDINATES: N44° 3.780' W92° 2.596'

CAMPING ALTERNATIVE: CARLEY STATE PARK

If Whitewater Park is too crowded, check out Carley State Park. Only about 20 minutes northwest of Whitewater, it offers 20 campsites (open Memorial Day–Labor Day) in a pleasant setting of maples, oaks, and pines. There are few amenities besides a short hiking trail, but the peace and quiet may be reward enough. Its proximity to Whitewater's treasure chest of natural attractions makes the short jaunt from campsite to park well worth it.

GETTING THERE: From I-90 take Exit 229, and head north on CR 10. In 12 miles the Carley State Park entrance is on the left.

GPS COORDINATES: N44° 6.597' W92° 10.175'

POSTSCRIPT

Although I did include a few campsites that are officially walk-in sites, none was really that far from the road—a basic criterion for a book featuring drive-up, family-camping opportunities. However, the campgrounds described below, all in state parks, have particularly noteworthy walk-in sites.

Afton State Park, a few miles southeast of downtown Saint Paul, is spread out amid the hills on the western bank of the St. Croix River. The only campground in this park is a mile or two from the parking area, with each campsite laid out in a large pocket of grass on a high, tree-flanked knoll. Great hiking awaits campers here.

George H. Crosby Manitou State Park is wonderful for backpack camping in Minnesota. Rocky, high-country North Shore terrain and cascading and sheer-drop waterfalls set the scene for small, intimate, and minimalist campsites along a trail network. Crosby Manitou offers near-wilderness camping in fantastic surroundings.

In Frontenac State Park, there are beautiful vistas from high atop a bluff overlooking the Mississippi at the head of Lake Pepin in southeastern Minnesota. While the campground is adequate, I think the best camping is available at the accessible walk-in sites down and across the road; these are tucked along the edge of an oak forest that borders a hilly area covered in prairie grasses and sumac. The extra effort you spend finding a cool campsite at one of the walk-ins will be rewarded by great scenery and the hikes along the bluffs and shoreline.

Lake Maria State Park is barely beyond the northernmost suburbs of the Twin Cities. It, too, is a great park for hiking but unfortunately does not offer a drive-in campground. Instead it has several sites, each securely nestled in the hardwood forests that cover the area. Each campsite is reached via a spur off the main hiking trail, and each sits beneath maples and oaks. The open understory makes these sites a bit less private than the others mentioned, but the setting and overall charm of this park make it all worthwhile.

APPENDIX A:

CAMPING EQUIPMENT CHECKLIST

The basic utensils and smaller items I routinely use on camping trips are conveniently packed in a large "camp kitchen" storage bin that transfers easily from garage to car in seconds. It makes preparing for a camping trip efficient. All I have to do is grab it along with my tent and sleeping bag, gather food to bring, and away I go. If I don't have it when I get to my campsite, I figure I really didn't need it in the first place. Some of the basic items I carry are:

COOKING IMPLEMENTS
Aluminum foil
Biodegradable dish soap
Bottle opener/corkscrew
Coffeepot
Containers of salt, pepper, other favorite
    seasonings, cooking oil, sugar
Cups, dishes, bowls
Frying pan (cast iron)
Fuel for camp stove
Large water container (wide mouth for filling;
    spigot for tapping)
Lighter, matches, and so on
Pots with lids (at least two: large and medium)
Small campstove (with wind guard)
Utensils, including big spoon, spatula, paring knife

FIRST AID KIT
Adhesive bandages (assorted sizes)
Acetaminophen or ibuprofen
Antibiotic cream (such as Neosporin)
Benadryl (or the generic equivalent,
    diphenhydramine)
Gauze pads
Insect repellent
Moleskin
Personal medications (dosages clearly marked)
Sunscreen/lip balm

SLEEPING GEAR
Pillow
Sleeping bag and liner (optional)
Sleeping pad (inflatable or insulated)
Tent with tub floor; tent fly; floor/ground tarp

MISCELLANEOUS
Bath soap (biodegradable)
Batteries/solar recharging unit
Camera and memory card with charger or
    batteries
Camp chair/hammock
Candles
Cooler
Deck of cards
Duct tape
Fire starter
Flashlight or headlamp with fresh batteries
Inclement-weather clothing
Paper towels
Plastic zip-top bags
Sunglasses
Toilet paper/hand sanitizer
Water bottle
Wool blanket

OPTIONAL
Barbecue grill
Binoculars
Field guides
Fishing gear
Lantern or tent candles
Maps, charts, and other references
    and information

APPENDIX B:

SOURCES OF INFORMATION

The following is a partial list of agencies, associations, and organizations to call for information on outdoor recreation opportunities in Minnesota.

CHIPPEWA NATIONAL FOREST
218-335-8600; 218-335-8632 (TTY)
www.fs.usda.gov/chippewa

BLACKDUCK RANGER DISTRICT
218-835-4291

DEER RIVER RANGER DISTRICT
218-246-2133

WALKER RANGER DISTRICT
218-547-1044

DEPARTMENT OF NATURAL RESOURCES
651-296-6157; 888-MINNDNR (646-6367)
Reservations: 866-85-PARKS (72757) or tinyurl.com/mnspreservations

SUPERIOR NATIONAL FOREST
218-626-4300; 218-626-4399 (TTY)
www.fs.usda.gov/superior

GUNFLINT RANGER DISTRICT
218-387-1750 (voice and TTY)

KAWISHIWI RANGER DISTRICT
218-365-7600; 218-365-7602 (TTY)

LACROIX RANGER DISTRICT
218-666-0020 (voice and TTY)

LAURENTIAN RANGER DISTRICT
218-229-8800 (voice and TTY)

MARCELL RANGER DISTRICT
218-832-3161

TOFTE RANGER DISTRICT
218-663-7280 (voice and TTY)

INDEX

Page numbers in *italics* represent photos.

OPPOSITE: Honeymoon Overlook on the trail near the entrance to Flour Lake Campground (see page 33)

ABOUT THE AUTHOR

Tom Watson has enjoyed 30 years of camping in Minnesota, first as an Eagle Scout with Troop 22 in Minneapolis; later as a college student studying forest resource management at the University of Minnesota; and then throughout his life in various professions, including as a freelance writer specializing in outdoor subjects.

Tom is an avid sea kayaker, naturalist, and photographer. He is also the author of *60 Hikes Within 60 Miles: Minneapolis and St. Paul* and *Best Minnesota Camper Cabins.*

DEAR CUSTOMERS AND FRIENDS,

SUPPORTING YOUR INTEREST IN OUTDOOR ADVENTURE, travel, and an active lifestyle is central to our operations, from the authors we choose to the locations we detail to the way we design our books. Menasha Ridge Press was incorporated in 1982 by a group of veteran outdoorsmen and professional outfitters. For many years now, we've specialized in creating books that benefit the outdoors enthusiast.

Almost immediately, Menasha Ridge Press earned a reputation for revolutionizing outdoors- and travel-guidebook publishing. For such activities as canoeing, kayaking, hiking, backpacking, and mountain biking, we established new standards of quality that transformed the whole genre, resulting in outdoor-recreation guides of great sophistication and solid content. Menasha Ridge Press continues to be outdoor publishing's greatest innovator.

The folks at Menasha Ridge Press are as at home on a whitewater river or mountain trail as they are editing a manuscript. The books we build for you are the best they can be, because we're responding to your needs. Plus, we use and depend on them ourselves.

We look forward to seeing you on the river or the trail. If you'd like to contact us directly, visit us at menasharidge.com. We thank you for your interest in our books and the natural world around us all.

SAFE TRAVELS,

Bob Sehlinger

BOB SEHLINGER
PUBLISHER